NETWORKING MASTERY

The Essential Guide to Networking Success

**A Comprehensive Guide to
Networking in the Modern Professional World**

CONTENTS

"The richest people in the world look for and build networks; everyone else looks for work."

Robert Kiyosaki

THE ACCIDENTAL NETWORKER

If someone had told me three decades ago that networking would become one of the most critical skills in my professional life, I might have smiled politely but been skeptical. Back then, "networking" wasn't the buzzword it is today, but I quickly learned it was key to thriving in business and international trade. As a newly promoted executive attending my first major industry conference, I'll admit—I felt a bit out of my depth. Surrounded by industry veterans and leaders who all seemed to know each other, I felt like the odd one out.

I stood back, taking in the room and mentally preparing myself to engage. The task felt daunting, but I knew that if I didn't start building connections, I'd be missing a key opportunity to grow professionally.

So, I took a deep breath and approached a group that was in the middle of a conversation about industry trends. I won't pretend it was a seamless introduction—I was nervous and stumbled a bit at first. But then, one of the professionals asked about my experience, and just like that, the conversation opened up. We discussed challenges in our fields, shared a few insights, and by the end of the night, I had exchanged business cards with several people.

What I learned that night was that networking isn't about being the most confident person in the room or dazzling everyone with what you know. It's about showing up, being genuine, and creating authentic connections. Those initial contacts? They turned into long-term business relationships, some of which I still maintain today.

Over the past 35 years, I've owned and led businesses across multiple sectors—human resources, technology, marketing, communications, and international trade and investment. Through it all, I've found that success comes from building relationships and nurturing them over time. Networking isn't just about making connections—it's about staying connected, being reliable, and showing up for people when it matters. Whether it's fostering trade opportunities or leading organizations, I've always believed that strong relationships are the foundation of any successful endeavor.

What's helped me throughout my career is a simple but essential approach: keep your word, deliver what you promise, and follow up when you say you will. People remember those who are dependable, who genuinely care about maintaining the connection. And that's the real key to networking—it's not about collecting contacts, it's about creating relationships that last.

"Your network is your net worth."

Porter Gale

CHAPTER 1

INTRODUCTION TO NETWORKING

WHAT IS NETWORKING?

Networking is the art of building genuine relationships with others that extend beyond just professional or social connections; it's about creating a community where both parties can exchange value, support each other's growth, and open doors to new opportunities. It's not just about who you know, but how you connect and interact with others to create long-term, mutually beneficial relationships.

Here's what networking is not:

- **Networking is not: Boasting About Achievements.** You know that person who starts every conversation with, "Let me tell you about my recent promotion"? That's not networking; that's just being *that person.* Networking is about mutual exchange, not a one-sided monologue.

- **Networking is not: Forced Friendships.** You're not required to become best friends with everyone you meet. Networking is about professional connections that may or may not evolve into friendships. If you click, great! If not, it's okay to keep it professional.

- **Networking is not: A Numbers Game.** Collecting contacts just to boost your LinkedIn connections or Facebook friends list doesn't count. Quality over quantity is the name of the game.

Why Network? Unlocking the True Power of Connections

When you hear the word "networking," what comes to mind? For many, it's visions of awkward cocktail parties, forced small talk, or a stack of business cards gathering dust in a drawer. It's easy to think of networking as just another chore—something you're supposed to do, but maybe don't really see the value in. But what if I told you that networking is so much more than just swapping business cards and awkward introductions?

Networking is one of the most powerful tools at your disposal, and it goes far beyond what you might expect. Let's break it down.

Networking Isn't Just About Who You Know—It's About What You Know

You've likely heard the saying, "It's not just what you know, but who you know." While there's certainly some truth to that, the real value lies in the combination of both. Networking isn't simply about meeting people; it's about building relationships that allow for the exchange of knowledge, ideas, and insights—things you might not have access to on your own.

Think of it this way: every person you meet has a unique set of experiences, skills, and perspectives. By connecting with them, you open yourself up fresh ways of thinking, and solutions to challenges you might not have considered. Networking can introduce you to mentors who guide you, peers who challenge you, and collaborators who help you achieve your

6

goals. It's like expanding your personal and professional toolbox—every new connection adds another tool that can help you succeed.

It's Not Just for Extroverts—It's for Everyone

One of the biggest misconceptions about networking is that it's only for extroverts—those who thrive in social situations and love meeting new people. But the truth is, networking is for everyone, no matter your personality type. You don't have to be the life of the party to be a successful networker. In fact, some of the most effective networkers are those who listen more than they talk, who build deep, one-on-one connections rather than working the room.

If you're an introvert, networking might look a little different for you. Maybe it's about attending smaller events, connecting with people online, or building relationships through shared interests rather than forced interactions. The key is to find a networking style that works for you—one that feels authentic and comfortable. Remember, the goal isn't to meet everyone in the room; it's to connect with people who resonate with you.

It's Not Just About Today—It's About Tomorrow

Networking isn't a one-and-done activity; it's an ongoing process that pays dividends over time. The connections you make today can lead to opportunities tomorrow, next year, or even a decade down the line. Maybe the person you met at that conference last month doesn't have anything to offer you right now, but a few years down the road, they might be the key to a major career opportunity—or vice versa.

Think of networking as planting seeds. You might not see the results right away, but with time, care, and attention, those seeds can grow into something significant. The relationships you build through networking are investments in your future, and the more you nurture them, the more they'll grow.

INTERACTIVE ELEMENT: QUICK SELF-ASSESSMENT

Before we get into the finer details of building your networking prowess, let's start with a little self-reflection. Think of this as your networking check-in—a chance to gauge where you're at, what's working, and where you might want to fine-tune your approach. No awkward small talk required, just an honest look at your current networking habits.

1. **How often do you attend networking events (in-person or online)?**

    A. Regularly (at least once a month) – You're basically the Beyoncé of networking.

    B. Occasionally (a few times a year) – Not bad, but room for improvement!

    C. Rarely (once a year or less) – We need to change that.

    D. Never – Don't worry, we're going to fix this.

2. **How comfortable are you in initiating conversations with new people?**

    A. Very comfortable – You're a natural-born networker.

    B. Somewhat comfortable – You've got potential.

    C. Uncomfortable – It's okay, practice makes perfect.

    D. Very uncomfortable – Don't worry, we'll turn this around.

3. How would you describe your current network?

A. Diverse and expansive – You're the social butterfly of networking.

B. B. Fairly broad – You've got a solid base, but there's always room to grow.

C. Limited – Time to spread those wings.

D. Minimal – Let's start building!

4. What is your primary goal for networking?

A. Career advancement – You're on a mission.

B. Personal growth – You're all about self-improvement.

C. Expanding social circles – New friends are always welcome.

D. Learning and development – The more you know, the more you grow.

5. How do you typically follow up after meeting someone new?

A. I reach out within a few days with a message or email – Gold star for you!

B. I connect with them on social media but don't always follow up directly – Not bad, but let's get proactive.

C. I wait for them to contact me first – We can work on that.

D. . I often forget to follow up – We've got some work to do!

SELF-ASSESSMENT RESULTS: WHERE DO YOU STAND?

1. The Networking Prodigy

Score: Mostly A's

Overview: You're already a networking champ. You've got a diverse network, and you follow up like a pro.

Next Steps: Keep refining your skills. Look for advanced tips to take your game to the next level.

2. The Budding Networker

Score: Mostly B's

Overview: You're comfortable with networking but still have room to grow.

Next Steps: Focus on deepening your connections and exploring new networking opportunities.

3. The Reluctant Networker

Score: Mostly C's

Overview: Networking isn't your favorite, but you're willing to try.

Next Steps: Start small. Pick one or two tips from this book to build your confidence.

4. The Networking Newbie

Score: Mostly D's

Overview: Networking is new or challenging for you.

Next Steps: Don't worry! This book will guide you through the basics, one step at a time.

Take a moment to reflect on your answers. No matter where you're starting from, this book will help you level up your networking game. Ready? Let's do this!

"In a world that is constantly changing, staying connected with others is the key to adaptation and success."

Brian Solis

CHAPTER 2

ADAPTING TO CONNECT

NETWORKING IN A FLEXIBLE WORK WORLD

As the landscape of work continues to evolve, so too does the way we approach networking. In today's workplace, the traditional office setting is no longer the default. With hybrid and remote work environments becoming the norm, professionals are enjoying newfound flexibility and autonomy. However, this shift also presents unique challenges—especially when it comes to networking. Gone are the days of impromptu hallway conversations, casual coffee breaks, and spontaneous brainstorming sessions by the water cooler. These moments, which once played a significant role in building relationships and sparking new ideas, are now few and far between.

Yet, the importance of networking hasn't diminished; in fact, it's more crucial than ever. Networking in a hybrid or remote setting isn't just about staying connected with your colleagues or maintaining your professional presence—it's about ensuring that you continue to grow, learn, and find new opportunities in an increasingly digital world.

Why Networking Matters More Than Ever

Working from home offers undeniable perks—no commute, greater work-life balance, and the ability to create a personalized workspace. But it also comes with a downside: the potential for isolation. Without the daily interactions that come naturally in a physical office, it's easy to feel disconnected from your peers and the broader professional community. This is where networking steps in, filling the gap left by the absence of in-person interactions.

Networking provides a platform for meaningful engagement. It keeps you informed about industry trends, introduces you to new perspectives, and fosters relationships that can support both your career development and personal growth. Engaging with others helps you stay energized and motivated, ensuring that you're not just going through the motions but actively participating in the larger professional ecosystem.

The Social Aspect of Networking

Humans are inherently social creatures. We thrive on connections, and our professional success is often tied to the relationships we build along the way. Networking isn't just a tool for climbing the career ladder; it's also essential for our social well-being. In a remote or hybrid work environment, making the effort to network is a way to step out of your daily routine, meet new people, and engage in conversations that spark creativity and inspire new ways of thinking.

Through networking, you can find mentors who guide you, collaborators who challenge you, and friends who support you—not just professionally, but personally as well. These relationships enrich your life, providing a sense of community and belonging in a world where interactions are increasingly digital.

Making Networking Intentional

In a hybrid or remote work environment, networking requires intentional effort. It's no longer something that happens naturally in the flow of a workday; it's something you have to seek out and make time for. This might mean attending virtual conferences, joining professional groups or online communities, or simply reaching out to someone new via LinkedIn or email.

But while it might require more effort, the benefits of networking in a remote or hybrid setting are well worth it. It keeps you connected, supported, and engaged with the world beyond your immediate tasks. It opens doors to new ideas, partnerships, and growth opportunities, ensuring that you continue to thrive in your career, even from a distance.

Networking as a Lifeline

In the modern workplace, where interactions are increasingly digital and our physical presence is often limited, networking becomes a lifeline. It's not just about advancing your career—it's about maintaining a sense of community, purpose, and connection. So, whether you're attending a virtual happy hour, participating in an online forum, or sending a thoughtful message to a new contact, make networking a regular part of your routine. In doing so, you'll not only keep your career on track but also enrich your personal and professional life in ways that are invaluable in today's world.

FOUNDATIONS OF EFFECTIVE NETWORKING

Now that we've clarified what networking truly is, let's dive into how to do it right. Effective networking isn't just about meeting people; it's about building relationships that are meaningful, authentic, and beneficial for everyone involved. To achieve this, there are three core principles you need to embrace: be genuine, be intentional, and be consistent. These aren't just buzzwords—they're the foundation of networking that actually works, creating connections that last and opportunities that matter.

1. Be Genuine: The Power of Authenticity

People can spot insincerity a mile away. When you approach networking with a genuine interest in others—when you're truly curious about their stories, experiences, and goals—you build trust. Being genuine means showing up as your true self, without trying to impress or manipulate. It's about listening more than you speak, asking thoughtful questions, and engaging in conversations that go beyond the surface. When you're authentic, people are more likely to connect with you on a deeper level, and those connections are the ones that will endure.

2. Be Intentional: Purpose-Driven Networking

Effective networking isn't about collecting as many business cards as possible or attending every event you can find. It's about being purposeful with your time and energy. Know why you're networking and what you want to achieve. Whether you're looking to learn from others, find potential collaborators, or explore new career opportunities, having a clear purpose will guide your interactions and help you connect with the right people. When you're intentional, your networking efforts become more focused and productive, leading to connections that align with your goals.

3. Be Consistent: Building Relationships Over Time

Networking isn't a one-off event; it's an ongoing process. Consistency is key to maintaining and growing your network. This means staying in touch with the people you meet, following up on conversations, and offering help or resources when you can. It's about nurturing relationships over time, rather than expecting immediate results. By being consistent, you show that you value the relationship, and you keep yourself on the radar for future opportunities. Consistent effort leads to a network that's not only wide but also deep, filled with people who know and trust you.

By embracing these three principles — genuineness, intentionality, and consistency—you lay the groundwork for effective networking. It's not just about who you know; it's about how you know them and how you continue to build and sustain those relationships. This is the kind of networking that leads to real, lasting success.

Common Networking Challenges and How to Overcome Them

Networking is one of those things that everyone knows they should do, but few people feel entirely comfortable with. It can be a minefield of awkward moments, unmet expectations, and the occasional bout of sweaty palms. But here's the good news: you're not alone, and most of the common challenges can be overcome with a little strategy and a lot of patience. Let's break down some of the most common networking hurdles and how to tackle them head-on.

Overcoming Introversion

If the thought of entering a room full of strangers makes you want to curl up with a good book instead, you're probably more introverted than extroverted. And that's okay! Networking doesn't mean you have to transform into a social butterfly overnight. In fact, introverts often bring valuable qualities to networking—like the ability to listen deeply and build strong, one-on-one connections.

Strategy:

Play to your strengths. Instead of trying to be the life of the party, focus on creating a few meaningful connections. Think of it as a treasure hunt— your goal is to find a few gems, not collect as much glitter as possible. At your next networking event, aim to have three solid conversations rather than working the entire room. Come prepared with a few topics you're passionate about, which can help ease the anxiety of starting a conversation. And remember, networking doesn't have to mean big events; one-on-one coffee meetings or virtual chats can be just as effective.

Example:

Take Emily, an introverted software engineer who used to dread networking events like they were dentist appointments. Instead of forcing herself to attend every social gathering, Emily decided to focus on what she did best—deep, thoughtful conversations. At her next industry conference, she ditched the cocktail party and instead scheduled coffee breaks with a few key contacts she was genuinely interested in knowing better. Not only did this approach save her energy, but it also led to stronger, more meaningful connections. Emily realized that she didn't need to "network" the traditional way to be successful—she just needed to do it her way.

Dealing with Rejection

Ah, rejection—the inevitable pitfall of putting yourself out there. Whether it's a cold email that never gets a response, a handshake that feels a little too limp, or a conversation that fizzles out, rejection in networking can feel like a punch to the gut. But here's the thing: it's not about you. Really.

Strategy:

Don't take it personally. Easier said than done, I know, but here's a little secret: rejection usually has more to do with timing or circumstances than with you personally. People are busy, distracted, or just not in the right place to engage. When you encounter rejection, treat it like a bad date— learn from it, laugh it off, and move on. Use it as an opportunity to refine your approach. Maybe that email was a bit too formal, or maybe your timing was off. Whatever the case, don't let it get you down. Instead, give it some time and try again with a fresh angle. Persistence is key, but so is respecting others' space and time.

Example:

Let me share a time when I experienced the sting of rejection in networking. I had just returned from a major industry event, feeling on top of the world after making what I thought were some solid connections. One person in particular, a well-known figure in my field, seemed especially promising. So, I spent a good half-hour crafting the perfect follow-up email—professional, engaging, and enthusiastic. And then... silence. No response. Days went by, and my inbox stayed stubbornly empty.

Initially, I felt deflated. But after reflecting, I realized there could be countless reasons for the lack of response—perhaps they were overwhelmed with work or simply missed my email. Rather than let it discourage me, I took it as a learning moment. A few weeks later, I followed up again, this time referencing a new project I was working on that aligned with their interests. This time, I got a reply, and we ended up having a productive conversation.

The takeaway? Persistence, when paired with patience and a bit of empathy, can transform what feels like rejection into an unexpected opportunity.

Navigating Cultural Miscommunications

Cross-cultural networking adds an extra layer of complexity to the mix. You're not just navigating different personalities—you're also dealing with different communication styles, cultural norms, and even body language. It's like trying to dance with someone when you're both hearing different music. Misunderstandings are bound to happen, but they don't have to derail the relationship.

Strategy:

Do your homework. Understanding the cultural norms and communication styles of the people you're networking with is crucial. Think of it as learning the local language—it might be challenging at first, but it makes everything smoother in the long run. Practice active listening, and don't be afraid to ask clarifying questions if something isn't clear. If a miscommunication does occur, address it respectfully and use it as a learning moment. Cultural sensitivity and adaptability are your best friends here.

Example:

Let's revisit Sarah, the American executive who learned the hard way that rushing through a French business lunch could be a recipe for disaster. She flew to Paris, eager to seal the deal, and was blindsided when her French counterparts seemed more interested in discussing wine pairings than the contract at hand. Her attempts to speed things along were met with cold stares and, ultimately, a stalled negotiation. Realizing her mistake, Sarah decided to adapt. She put her agenda aside, embraced the leisurely pace, and focused on building rapport over the meal. By dessert, the ice had thawed, and the deal that had seemed on shaky ground was back on track. Sarah's takeaway? Sometimes, the fastest way to a deal is by slowing down and respecting the cultural context.

"Networking is not just about connecting people. It's about connecting people with people, people with ideas, and people with opportunities."

Michele Jennae

CHAPTER 3

FOUNDATIONS OF EFFECTIVE NETWORKING BEYOND EXCHANGES

Networking and socializing may appear similar on the surface, but there's a key distinction between the two. Socializing is what happens when you're at a gathering, engaging in light conversation about common interests. Networking, however, occurs when you recognize that the person you're speaking with shares professional interests or has potential value to your career, and you both stand to benefit from an exchange of ideas or information.

The most effective networking often feels seamless, blending naturally with social interaction. For instance, imagine you're at a casual event, discussing your favorite books with someone. As the conversation unfolds, you mention that you've always aspired to write. The person you're speaking with then reveals that they are an editor seeking new projects. Without forcing the conversation, you've transitioned from socializing to networking in a way that feels organic.

Consider another scenario: You're at a coffee meetup, and the conversation initially revolves around weekend plans. As you speak, you discover that your acquaintance works in an industry you've been interested in. Here, the opportunity arises to subtly guide the discussion toward your professional aspirations, asking a few thoughtful questions that could potentially lead to a valuable connection.

The art of blending networking with socializing lies in maintaining a natural flow. Rather than steering the conversation too abruptly into business matters, allow it to evolve there naturally. Observe cues from the other person—if they appear interested in discussing professional topics, proceed. If not, it's perfectly fine to keep the conversation light and explore the opportunity at a later time. At the same time, don't feel uncomfortable bringing the conversation to business. In most networking settings, people expect to talk shop, and it's a key reason everyone is there. The goal is to make that transition seamless, allowing it to feel like a natural progression in the conversation. Start by building rapport, finding common ground, or discussing shared interests. When the moment feels right, moving into business topics won't feel forced—it will be an extension of the connection you've already begun.

Quick Tip: How to Transition from Casual Conversation to Professional Opportunities

So, how do you make that smooth transition from talking about the latest movie to discussing potential collaborations without it feeling awkward? Here's a simple formula:

1. **Start with Common Ground:** Keep the conversation casual and find something you both enjoy or have in common. This builds rapport and makes the other person more receptive to what comes next.

2. **Drop a Subtle Hint:** Casually mention your professional interests or projects in a way that relates to the conversation. For example, if you're talking about a recent trip, you might say, "It was such a great experience—gave me a lot of inspiration for the marketing campaign I'm working on."

3. **Gauge Their Interest:** Pay attention to how they respond. If they show interest or ask follow-up questions, you've got the green light to dive deeper. If they seem disinterested, it's okay to leave it for another time.

4. **Transition Smoothly:** If they're interested, naturally steer the conversation towards opportunities. You might say, "By the way, I've been thinking about exploring more in that field—do you have any advice or know of any opportunities?"

5. **End on a High Note:** Whether or not the conversation turns into a professional opportunity, end on a positive, friendly note. This leaves the door open for future interactions.

THE RIGHT MINDSET FOR NETWORKING

Mastering the art of networking goes far beyond simply meeting people, exchanging handshakes, or swapping business cards. If it were only about these surface-level actions, everyone would excel at it. In reality, successful networking is driven by the mindset you bring to each interaction.

To truly thrive in this space, it's important to shift your focus from what you can gain to what you can give. Prioritizing a "giving first" approach not only makes you more approachable, but it also helps cultivate stronger, more genuine relationships that stand the test of time.

Why Mindset Matters in Networking

Many people approach networking with the mindset of gaining something—new contacts, job leads, or business opportunities. While these are important outcomes, focusing solely on personal gain can backfire. When others sense they're being seen as just a stepping stone, it can prevent the formation of real, meaningful connections. Instead, successful networking comes from genuine interest and mutual benefit, creating relationships that last.

Instead of thinking about what you'll gain from the interaction, consider how you can add value to the other person's life or work. This could be sharing your expertise, providing a useful resource, offering an introduction, or just being a supportive listener. When you prioritize helping others, you naturally become more approachable, setting the stage for genuine, meaningful connections.

The Power of a Giving Mindset

A giving mindset is powerful because it transforms the way people perceive you. When you're genuinely interested in helping others, you become someone who others want to be around and work with. This is because giving fosters trust, and trust is the foundation of any strong relationship. When people know that you're not just out to get something from them, they're more likely to open up, share their own insights, and look for ways to help you in return.

This approach also helps you stand out in a crowded networking environment. While many people may be focused on pushing their own agendas, you'll be the one who's remembered for your generosity and willingness to support others. And here's the best part: when you give without expecting anything in return, the rewards often come back to you in unexpected ways. Whether it's through a referral, a new opportunity, or simply the goodwill you've built up over time, giving creates a positive cycle that benefits everyone involved.

How to Cultivate a Giving Mindset

If you're used to thinking of networking in more transactional terms, shifting to a giving mindset might feel like a big change. But the good news is that it's a shift anyone can make with a little practice and intention. Here's how to get started:

1. **Focus on Building Relationships, Not Just Contacts:**

   Instead of viewing each interaction as a potential transaction, focus on building genuine relationships. Take the time to get to know people on a deeper level—what are their goals, challenges, and passions? How can you support them in what they're trying to achieve? By focusing on the relationship first, the benefits of networking will naturally follow.

2. **Be Curious and Ask Questions:**

   A key part of giving is understanding what others need. And the best way to do that is by being curious and asking questions. Instead of immediately jumping into what you do or what you need, start by asking about the other person. What are they working on? What challenges are they facing? What's most important to them right now? The more you know, the better equipped you'll be to offer meaningful support.

3. **Offer Help Without Strings Attached:**

   One of the most effective ways to cultivate a giving mindset is to offer help without expecting anything in return. This could be as simple as sharing a useful article, offering advice on a problem, or introducing them to someone in your network who could help. The key is to give freely, without any hidden agendas. When people see that your help comes with no strings attached, they're more likely to trust you and reciprocate in the future.

4. Celebrate Others' Successes:

Part of giving is recognizing and celebrating the successes of those in your network. Whether it's congratulating someone on a promotion, sharing their work on social media, or simply sending a note of encouragement, acknowledging others' achievements helps strengthen your relationships and shows that you're genuinely invested in their success.

5. Be a Connector:

One of the most valuable things you can give is a connection. If you know two people who could benefit from knowing each other, don't hesitate to introduce them. Whether it's connecting a job seeker with a potential employer or introducing two colleagues who share similar interests, being a connector is a powerful way to add value to your network.

The Long-Term Benefits of a Giving Mindset

While a giving mindset might not yield immediate results, it pays off in the long run. By consistently focusing on how you can help others, you build a reputation as someone who is trustworthy, reliable, and genuinely interested in the well-being of others. Over time, this reputation becomes one of your greatest assets, attracting new opportunities, connections, and collaborations.

Moreover, when you give generously, you create a positive ripple effect in your network. The people you help are more likely to help others in turn, creating a culture of support and collaboration that benefits everyone. And because you've built your network on a foundation of trust and mutual respect, the relationships you form are more likely to be enduring and fruitful.

Adopting the Right Mindset for Networking

Effective networking isn't just about the mechanics of meeting people; it's about adopting the right mindset—one that prioritizes giving over receiving. By focusing on how you can add value to others, you create stronger, more authentic relationships that stand the test of time. Remember, networking is a long game, and the relationships you build today through a giving mindset will pay dividends in the future.

As you continue to develop your networking skills, keep this mindset at the forefront of your interactions. Not only will it make networking more rewarding for you, but it will also make you a person that others are eager to connect with and support.

ETHICAL NETWORKING: WHAT IT MEANS AND WHY IT MATTERS

Networking is all about making connections—meeting people, building relationships, and creating opportunities. But like any powerful tool, networking comes with responsibilities. It's not just about who you know or how many contacts you can collect; it's about how you build and maintain those relationships in a way that's fair, honest, and respectful. This is where ethical networking comes into play.

What Is Ethical Networking?

Let's start with the basics. Ethical networking means conducting yourself with integrity in all your interactions. In other words, it's networking done right—not just to benefit yourself, but to create genuine, mutually beneficial relationships.

Picture this: You're at an industry conference, and you strike up a conversation with a senior executive from a company you admire.

Instead of diving straight into a pitch about how they could help you, you start by asking about their career journey, genuinely listening to their experiences and insights. Over the course of the conversation, you find common ground—perhaps you both started in similar roles or have faced similar challenges.

Rather than trying to immediately secure a favor, you offer to send an article or resource that might be helpful based on something they mentioned. This isn't about leveraging the person for your next opportunity; it's about establishing a meaningful connection rooted in mutual interest and respect. That's what ethical networking looks like—taking time to give before expecting anything in return, and showing genuine interest in who the person is, not just what they can offer you.

My Network: Real Stories and Lessons

At a marketing conference I attended, I had the opportunity to meet someone highly respected in the industry—let's call him John. With years of experience and an extensive network, John had access to opportunities I hadn't even considered. While it might have been tempting to see him as a stepping stone to the next big project, I knew that a transactional approach wouldn't lead to a meaningful or lasting connection.

Instead of diving straight into business talk, I took a different approach. We started by chatting about the keynote speaker, discovering a shared appreciation for their innovative ideas in digital marketing. From there, the conversation flowed naturally. John shared his insights on trends, and I focused on listening and adding thoughtful contributions. My goal wasn't to impress, but to build a genuine connection.

As time went on, our professional relationship grew, grounded in mutual respect. We kept in touch after the conference, exchanging ideas and collaborating on smaller projects. This connection opened doors to opportunities I wouldn't have had access to otherwise.

Our relationship was built on trust and authenticity, not on transactions. And that's the focus of this chapter—how cultivating real connections in networking can lead to long-term, valuable relationships that foster professional growth.

Why Is Ethical Networking Important?

Ethical networking is important for several reasons:

It Builds Trust:

Trust is the foundation of any strong relationship, professional or personal. When you conduct yourself ethically, people are more likely to trust you, which makes them more willing to help you, refer you to others, or collaborate with you in the future.

It Protects Your Reputation:

Your reputation is one of your most valuable assets in the professional world. If you're known as someone who uses others for personal gain or who cuts corners, that reputation will follow you—and not in a good way. Ethical networking ensures that your reputation remains positive, which can open more doors in the long run.

It Creates Long-Term Relationships:

Networking isn't just about short-term gains; it's about building relationships that can last for years. When you network ethically, you're more likely to form connections that are genuine and enduring. These are the kinds of relationships that can support you throughout your career, not just in the moment.

Common Ethical Dilemmas in Networking

Even with the best intentions, networking can sometimes lead to ethical dilemmas—situations where the line between right and wrong isn't always clear. Here are a few common examples:

1. **Quid Pro Quo Expectations:**

   Scenario: You help someone with a job lead, and they now expect to return the favor by doing something for you. While it's natural to want to reciprocate, ethical networking means that help should be offered freely, not because something is expected in return

   Solution: Make it clear that your assistance comes with no strings attached. Encourage a culture of giving without expecting anything in return. If someone insists on repaying the favor, suggest that they pay it forward by helping someone else in need.

2. **Misrepresenting Yourself:**

   Scenario: You're at a networking event, and you're tempted to exaggerate your skills or experience to impress someone.

   Solution: Always be honest about who you are and what you can do. It's better to be truthful about your abilities than to overpromise and underdeliver. Remember, authenticity is key in building trust.

3. **Overstepping Boundaries:**

   Scenario: You've developed a friendly rapport with a colleague, but now you're wondering if it's appropriate to ask for a professional favor.

   Solution: Be mindful of the stage of your relationship. If it's still new, focus on building the connection before making any requests. Overstepping too soon can damage the relationship rather than strengthen it

4. **Networking at the Expense of Others:**

    Scenario: You're at an event, and you see an opportunity to connect with someone influential, but it means sidelining a colleague who also wants to connect with that person.

    Solution: Ethical networking means being inclusive, not exclusive. Find a way to introduce your colleague or include them in the conversation. Networking should be about creating opportunities for everyone, not just yourself.

How to Practice Ethical Networking

Now that you understand what ethical networking is and why it's important, let's talk about how to practice it in your everyday interactions:

1. **Show Up Honestly:**

    Always be truthful about your intentions, abilities, and experiences. If you're looking to collaborate with someone, be upfront about what you're hoping to achieve and what you can offer in return.

2. **Respect Boundaries:**

    Understand that not every relationship will immediately lead to a business opportunity, and that's okay. Respect the other person's time and boundaries, and don't push too hard for favors or connections.

3. **Give Without Expecting in Return:**

    One of the hallmarks of ethical networking is the ability to give freely. Whether it's advice, a connection, or simply your time, offer your help without expecting anything in return. This approach not only builds trust but also creates a more positive and supportive network.

4. Protect Confidentiality:

In your networking interactions, you may come across sensitive information. Always respect the confidentiality of what is shared with you, and never use it to your advantage at someone else's expense.

5. Promote Inclusivity:

Ethical networking means looking out for others, not just yourself. If you see opportunities where someone else could benefit, don't hesitate to make introductions or share information. Helping others succeed is one of the most rewarding aspects of networking.

Navigating Networking with Integrity

Networking is often seen as the art of connection, but like any art, it comes with its own set of ethical considerations. The line between building genuine relationships and exploiting connections can sometimes blur, leading to dilemmas that challenge your integrity. But fear not! With a clear understanding of ethical practices, you can navigate these challenges with confidence and maintain your professional reputation.

Remember, ethical networking isn't just about following a set of rules about adopting a mindset that prioritizes fairness, respect, and mutual benefit. By practicing ethical networking, you not only build stronger, more authentic relationships but also create a network that's based on trust and long-term success. So as you continue to grow your network, let integrity be your guide, and watch as your connections thrive in a positive, supportive environment.

CHECKLIST: ETHICAL NETWORKING PRACTICES

Networking is like a dance—you want to make sure you're moving in sync with your partner, not stepping on any toes. To help you keep your moves smooth and ethical, here's a fun, interactive checklist you can use to ensure you're staying on the right track. Let's see how you're doing!

1. **The Honesty Test**

   Have you ever exaggerated your skills or experience to impress someone?

   ☐ Nope, I keep it real.

   ☐ Maybe once or twice... but I'm working on it!

   ☐ Gulp... okay, I need to tone it down.

   Do you clearly communicate your intentions when networking?

   ☐ Always! I'm as clear as crystal.

   ☐ Sometimes, but I could be clearer.

   ☐ Honestly, I'm kind of vague.

2. **The Reciprocity Radar**

   Do you offer help without expecting anything in return?

   ☐ Absolutely! I'm all about giving.

   ☐ I try, but it's hard not to expect something back.

   ☐ If I help, I want something in return.

When someone helps you, do you feel obligated to repay them immediately?

☐   Not really, I believe in paying it forward.

☐   Sometimes, I feel the pressure to return the favor.

☐   Definitely, I feel like I owe them.

3. **The Boundary Balancer**

Do you respect others' time and boundaries when networking?

☐   Yep, I always make sure not to overstep.

☐   I try, but sometimes I push a little too hard.

☐   I tend to overreach—I need to back off.

Do you wait until a relationship is established before asking for favors?

☐   Absolutely, I let the relationship grow first.

☐   It depends on the situation.

☐   I've been known to ask a bit too early.

4. **The Inclusivity Indicator**

When you see an opportunity that could benefit someone else, do you share it?

☐   Always! I love helping others succeed.

☐   I do, but sometimes I hesitate.

☐   Honestly, I keep it to myself most of the time.

Do you make an effort to include others in conversations or opportunities?

☐   Yep, I'm all about inclusivity!

☐   Sometimes, but I could do more.

☐   I tend to focus on myself first.

5. **The Confidentiality Check**

Do you respect the confidentiality of the information shared with you?

☐   Always—my lips are sealed.

☐   I try, but I've slipped a few times.

☐   Oops... I've shared things I shouldn't have.

Would others describe you as trustworthy with sensitive information?

☐   Definitely, I'm known for being discreet.

☐   I think so, but I'm not sure.

☐   Probably not, I need to work on this.

How Did You Do?

☐ Mostly A's: You're an ethical networking superstar! Keep doing what you're doing—you're building strong, trustworthy relationships that will serve you well in the long run.

☐ Mostly B's: You're on the right track, but there's room for improvement. Focus on tightening up those areas where you might be slipping a bit. Remember, it's all about consistency.

☐ Mostly C's: It's time to rethink your approach. Ethical networking is crucial for long-term success, so consider making some changes to ensure you're building relationships the right way. Start small, and work on one area at a time.

Use this checklist as a fun way to keep yourself accountable and ensure you're practicing ethical networking in every interaction. After all, the best connections are built on trust, respect, and integrity!

READY TO PRACTICE?

Now that you're equipped with insights, it's time to put your networking skills into action. Here are a few straightforward steps you can take today to begin building and strengthening your connections:

Action Step: Immediate Networking Actions

1. **Reconnect with an Old Contact**: Think of someone in your network you haven't spoken to in a while—a former colleague, mentor, or client. Send a message with a personal touch, like, "Hi [Name], I was reflecting on our last conversation about [topic] and wanted to check in. How have things been for you lately? Let's catch up!" It's a simple way to re-ignite old connections and stay relevant in your network.

2. **Join an Online Group or Forum**: Explore a professional group or community related to your industry or interests. Whether on LinkedIn or elsewhere, introduce yourself and contribute to the conversation. Share an article, answer a question, or offer a perspective. Being active in online spaces positions you as someone engaged and open to building new relationships.

3. **Attend a Networking Event or Webinar**: Find an upcoming industry event—whether it's local or virtual. Set a goal for yourself, like meeting one new person or asking a thoughtful question during the event. These small commitments can lead to big opportunities, from new collaborations to professional partnerships.

4. **Offer Help to Someone in Your Network**: Think of a colleague or connection who might benefit from a kind gesture. Whether it's sharing advice, making an introduction, or simply lending a listening

ear, offer support with sincerity. For example, "I remember you're working on [project] and thought you might find this resource helpful." Helping others strengthens your relationships and positions you as a valuable contact.

5. **Update Your Professional Profiles**: Refresh your LinkedIn or any other professional profiles. Ensure your latest accomplishments and skills are listed and that your profile clearly reflects your current role and value. First impressions matter — even in the digital space. When someone looks you up, your profile should communicate who you are and what you offer.

6. **Reach Out to a New Connection**: Take the plunge and message someone you've recently met, or who you admire from afar. It could be as simple as, "I've been following your work on [topic] and would love to connect. I think we have some shared interests, and I'd enjoy learning more about your perspective." It's a friendly, non-intimidating way to grow your network.

7. **Share a Personal Win or Insight on Social Media**: Post something insightful on LinkedIn, Twitter, or another platform you're comfortable with. Share a lesson you've learned recently, a milestone you've achieved, or an article that resonated with you. It's a great way to spark engagement and invite others into the conversation without having to directly reach out first.

8. **Send a Thank-You Note**: If someone in your network has recently helped or inspired you, send a brief thank-you email (or even an handwritten note). It doesn't need to be long — just a simple note of appreciation can go a long way in nurturing relationships. "Thanks for your advice on [topic] the other day — it's really helped me rethink my approach, and I'm grateful for your support!"

9. **Ask for Feedback**: Reach out to someone you trust for feedback on a current project or professional challenge. Asking for advice not only opens up a conversation but also shows that you value their opinion, strengthening your connection. "I'd love your thoughts on [project]—I know you have experience in this area, and any insight would be hugely appreciated."

"You don't have to be great to start, but you have to start to be great."

Zig Ziglar

CHAPTER 4

THE ART OF NETWORKING

NETWORKING WITH CONFIDENCE: WHY YOU'VE GOT THIS (AND HOW TO BUILD IT IF YOU DON'T)

Let's be honest—networking can be intimidating. The thought of walking up to a stranger, striking up a conversation, and trying to make a good impression can make even the most outgoing person feel a little nervous. But here's the thing: confidence is the secret sauce that makes networking not just possible, but successful. And guess what? You already have plenty of reasons to be confident.

Why Confidence Matters in Networking

Confidence isn't just a nice-to-have in networking—it's a game-changer. When you approach others with confidence, you're more likely to spark meaningful conversations, make a lasting impression, and build stronger connections. Why? Because confidence is contagious. When you project it, people are naturally drawn to you, more inclined to listen, trust, and see you as someone worth knowing.

Here's an even more compelling reason to embrace confidence: research shows that it's often perceived as competence. In other words, appearing confident makes others view you as capable and knowledgeable—even if you're still learning. This can profoundly impact how you're perceived in professional settings, making it easier to foster connections and unlock new opportunities.

You Already Have What It Takes

Now, you might be thinking, "But I'm not a naturally confident person. What if I don't have what it takes?" Well, here's the good news: you absolutely do. Confidence doesn't mean being the loudest person in the room or having all the answers. It's about believing in your own value, your abilities, and what you have to offer. And trust me, you have plenty to offer.

Think about the skills, experiences, and unique perspectives you bring to the table. Maybe you're a great listener, a problem-solver, or someone who's always willing to lend a hand. These qualities are just as important in networking as being a smooth talker or having a flashy job title. The key is to recognize your own strengths and let them shine through in your interactions with others.

I'll always remember the first time I truly stumbled in a networking situation. I was at a high-profile industry mixer, eager to connect with potential partners and clients. As a business owner, making the right connections was crucial for growing my company. I had meticulously prepared my pitch, ready to highlight the innovative solutions my business offered.

When the moment finally came to introduce myself, I was so focused on delivering my pitch flawlessly that I forgot to engage with the executive. I blurted out my company's achievements, my future goals, and what I could bring to the table. But I didn't take a moment to ask about their interests, their challenges, or what they were looking for. I was so wrapped up in my own agenda that I missed the chance to build a genuine connection.

The executive listened politely, but I could tell I hadn't struck the chord I was hoping for. After that encounter, I felt deflated, but I also learned a crucial lesson: networking isn't just about selling your own story. It's about creating a dialogue, understanding the other person's needs, and finding common ground. That experience taught me to approach networking with curiosity and collaboration, rather than just focusing on self-promotion.

This lesson is valuable for anyone, not just business owners. Whether you're looking to advance your career or build personal connections, the key is to engage meaningfully, listen actively, and foster genuine relationships. It's about making connections that matter, not just ticking off your networking to-do list.

If you're still building your confidence, don't worry—you're not alone. Confidence is a skill, and like any skill, it can be developed over time. The more you practice networking, the more comfortable you'll become, and the easier it will be to project confidence, even if you're feeling a bit nervous on the inside.

Here's how to get started:

1. Prepare Ahead of Time:

One of the best ways to boost your confidence is to prepare. Before attending a networking event, take some time to research who will be there, what topics might come up, and how you can contribute to the conversation. Having a few talking points ready will make you feel more in control and less likely to freeze up when the time comes to speak.

2. Focus on What You Can Control:

You can't control how others will respond, but you can control your own actions and attitude. Focus on being present, listening actively, and engaging genuinely with others. When you shift your focus away from worrying about what others think and toward being the best version of yourself, your confidence will naturally start to build.

3. Practice Positive Self-Talk:

The way you talk to yourself matters. Instead of dwelling on your insecurities, remind yourself of your strengths and what you bring to the table. Simple affirmations like "I have valuable insights to share" or "I'm capable of forming meaningful connections" can go a long way in boosting your confidence.

4. Start Small:

If the idea of walking up to a group of strangers at a large networking event feels overwhelming, start with smaller, more manageable interactions. Maybe it's reaching out to a colleague you haven't spoken to in a while or introducing yourself to someone new at a smaller gathering. Each successful interaction will build your confidence and prepare you for bigger networking opportunities.

5. Embrace the Learning Process:

No one becomes a networking pro overnight, and that's okay. Every interaction is a chance to learn, grow, and improve. Instead of focusing on the outcome of each conversation, focus on what you can learn from the experience. Over time, you'll find that your confidence grows with each new interaction.

CONFIDENCE: THE KEY TO MAKING A LASTING IMPRESSION

Here's the bottom line: confidence is what enables you to approach others, engage in meaningful conversations, and leave a lasting impression. It's not about being perfect or knowing everything—it's about showing up as your authentic self and trusting that you have something valuable to offer. And the best part? The more you practice, the more your confidence will grow.

So, the next time you find yourself doubting your ability to network effectively, remember this: you've got this. You already have the skills, experiences, and qualities that make you worth knowing. And if you're still working on your confidence, that's okay—there's always time to develop new skills and grow into the confident networker you're meant to be.

Now that you're ready to approach networking with confidence, it's time to equip yourself with one of the most powerful tools in your arsenal: the elevator pitch. This brief, persuasive speech can help you make a strong first impression and open doors to new opportunities. Let's dive into what an elevator pitch is, why it's so important, and how you can craft one that truly stands out.

What Exactly Is an Elevator Pitch?

Let's break it down. Imagine you step into an elevator, and right there with you is someone you've been dying to connect with—maybe it's a potential client, a future boss, or someone who could be a great collaborator. You have their undivided attention, but only for the duration of that elevator ride, which might be 30 to 60 seconds. That's your window of opportunity to make an impression and spark their interest.

An elevator pitch is essentially a mini-speech that you've prepared in advance for just this kind of situation. It's a brief, persuasive summary of who you are, what you do, and what makes you or your idea stand out. The goal is to grab the other person's attention quickly and make them want to know more about you. Think of it as your verbal business card—a quick way to introduce yourself that leaves a lasting impression.

Why Do You Need an Elevator Pitch?

Now, you might be thinking, "Why do I need a pitch? Can't I just introduce myself the usual way?" Well, here's the thing: In networking, first impressions are everything, and sometimes you only have a few seconds to make one. An elevator pitch helps you make the most of those precious moments. Instead of fumbling for words or giving a long-winded explanation that loses the other person's interest, you can deliver a clear, concise message that immediately communicates your value.

Having an elevator pitch prepared also boosts your confidence. It gives you something to fall back on when you're nervous or unsure of what to say. And because it's short and to the point, it helps you stay focused on the key points you want to convey, making you sound more professional and polished. In short, an elevator pitch is your secret weapon for making a strong impression quickly.

How to Create a Winning Elevator Pitch

Creating an effective elevator pitch might seem intimidating, but it's actually pretty straightforward once you break it down. Here's a simple formula to help you craft a pitch that works:

1. **Start with a Hook:**

   Your first sentence should grab the listener's attention. This is your chance to make them curious about who you are and what you do. The hook could be a bold statement, an intriguing question, or a surprising fact related to your work. For example, "I help small businesses triple their online sales in just six months" immediately makes the listener think, "Wow, how do they do that?"

2. Explain What You Do:

Next, give a brief explanation of what you do. Keep it simple and avoid jargon—this should be understandable even to someone who isn't in your field. For instance, if you're a graphic designer, you might say, "I'm a graphic designer who specializes in creating eye-catching websites that help businesses stand out."

3. Highlight What Makes You Unique:

This is where you differentiate yourself from others. What sets you apart? What's your unique selling point? Maybe it's your years of experience, a special skill, or a unique approach you take in your work. For example, "Unlike other designers, I focus on minimalist designs that are both beautiful and functional, which has helped my clients increase user engagement by 50%."

4. End with a Call to Action:

Finally, wrap up your pitch with a call to action. This is what you want the other person to do next—whether it's scheduling a meeting, visiting your website, or simply exchanging contact information. For example, "I'd love to discuss how I can help your company enhance its online presence. Do you have time for a coffee next week?"

Practice Makes Perfect

Once you've crafted your elevator pitch, it's time to practice. The more you rehearse, the more natural it will feel, and the easier it will be to deliver confidently when the moment arises. Practice in front of a mirror, with a friend, or even record yourself to see how you come across. The goal is to be able to deliver your pitch smoothly, without sounding rehearsed or robotic.

It's also a good idea to have a few variations of your pitch ready, depending on who you're speaking to. For example, you might have one version for potential clients, another for industry peers, and a third for casual networking events. The core message will be the same, but you can tweak the details to suit the audience and the situation.

Why It's Worth the Effort

You might be wondering if it's really worth putting in all this effort for a pitch that's only 30 seconds long. The answer is a resounding yes. In networking, those 30 seconds can make all the difference. A well-crafted elevator pitch can open doors to new opportunities, whether it's landing a new client, getting a job interview, or forming a valuable connection. It's an investment in your professional success, and like any good investment, it pays off.

So, take the time to create an elevator pitch that truly represents you and what you have to offer. Practice it until it feels natural, and use it confidently the next time you're in a networking situation. You never know when those 30 seconds might lead to something big.

ELEVATOR PITCH BUILDER CHECKLIST

Creating an elevator pitch that sticks is like crafting a perfect recipe—you need the right ingredients in the right amounts. Use this checklist to whip up a pitch that's sure to impress:

1. Start with a Hook:

☐ Does your opening line grab attention like a plot twist in a thriller?

☐ Is it intriguing enough to make someone want to know more?

2. Clearly Explain What You Do:

☐ Have you nailed down your role in a way that even your grandma would understand?

☐ Is it free of confusing jargon that could make eyes glaze over?

3. Highlight Your Unique Selling Proposition (USP):

☐ Does your pitch showcase what makes you the secret sauce in your industry?

☐ Are you highlighting your unique value like a rare gem?

4. Mention Your Goal or Call to Action:

☐ Have you made it clear what you want out of the conversation?

☐ Is there a smooth call to action that invites the listener to take the next step?

5. Keep It Brief and Clear:

☐ Is your pitch short enough to deliver before the elevator reaches the top floor?

☐ Have you stripped out any fluff that might cloud your message?

6. Practice and Refine:

☐ Have you practiced until it rolls off your tongue like your favorite song lyrics?

☐ Are you ready to deliver it with confidence, no matter the audience?

With this checklist in hand, you'll craft an elevator pitch that's not just good—it's unforgettable.

"To be interesting, be interested."

Dale Carnegie

CHAPTER 5

UNLOCKING THE POWER OF CASUAL CONVERSATIONS

THE SECRET POWER OF SMALL TALK: WHY CHITCHAT MATTERS MORE THAN YOU THINK

Small talk often gets a bad reputation. You've likely heard people dismiss it as trivial or unproductive. After all, why would you want to chat about the weather or last night's TV show when there are more pressing business matters to discuss? Isn't networking about forging meaningful connections rather than engaging in surface-level conversation?

Surprisingly, though, small talk is one of the most powerful tools in your networking toolkit. Far from being meaningless filler, it serves as the essential first step toward building rapport. Think of it as the warm-up before the main event—a way to ease into more substantial conversations. By mastering the art of small talk, you open the door to deeper, more meaningful connections.

Why Small Talk Matters

Let's start by debunking a common myth: small talk isn't pointless. In fact, it serves a critical function in the art of communication, especially in networking. Think of small talk as the appetizer before a meal. You wouldn't walk into a fancy restaurant and demand the main course before even sitting down, right? The same goes for conversations. Jumping straight into heavy topics without any warm-up can feel abrupt and uncomfortable for everyone involved.

Small talk eases the tension, breaks the ice, and creates a comfortable atmosphere where people feel more at ease. It's a way of signaling that you're approachable, friendly, and interested in others—not just in what they can do for you. And when people feel comfortable, they're more likely to open up, share more meaningful information, and be receptive to deeper conversations.

Using Small Talk to Open Doors at Networking Events

Jake, a young entrepreneur with big dreams and a pressing need for funding, found himself at his first major networking mixer. The event was a high-energy affair, filled with seasoned investors, accomplished business moguls, and the faint clatter of too many shrimp cocktails. With the future of his startup on the line, Jake knew he needed to make a meaningful connection, but the prospect of approaching potential investors felt daunting.

As Jake scanned the room, he noticed a well-known investor—a sharp dresser who was deeply engaged in conversation with a small group near the bar. This was someone with a reputation for backing innovative startups, but also for being difficult to impress. Jake took a deep breath, straightened his tie, and decided to seize the opportunity. Instead of launching into a rehearsed pitch, however, he remembered some sage advice: sometimes the best way to break the ice isn't with a business pitch, but with a bit of small talk.

Standing near the bar, Jake overheard the investor discussing a recent championship game that had captivated sports fans everywhere. Recognizing his opening, Jake casually chimed in, reflecting on how thrilling the game had been and expressing his amazement at the dramatic comeback. The investor, clearly pleased to find someone who shared his enthusiasm for sports, engaged with Jake easily. They discussed the game, the players, and their favorite teams, quickly establishing a friendly rapport.

With the conversation flowing smoothly, Jake found a natural moment to steer the topic towards his startup. He compared the ups and downs of his entrepreneurial journey to the twists and turns of the game they had just discussed, highlighting his persistence and recent successes. The investor, now intrigued, listened attentively as Jake explained his vision and the milestone his startup had recently achieved.

By focusing first on a shared interest, Jake managed to build a connection that felt genuine rather than transactional. The investor, now seeing Jake as more than just another pitch in the room, began asking questions and offering advice. What started as casual small talk about a sports event had seamlessly transitioned into a meaningful discussion about Jake's business.

A week later, Jake received an email from the investor, expressing interest in learning more about his startup. What had begun as a simple, informal conversation at a crowded networking mixer had opened the door to a potential investment opportunity—all because Jake used small talk to break the ice and build rapport before diving into business.

Building Trust Through Small Talk

Here's something else to consider: small talk is a trust-building tool. Before someone is willing to dive into a serious business discussion or share valuable insights, they need to feel like they can trust you. Small talk is how you lay the groundwork for that trust. It's a way to show that you're not just all business, that you're human, and that you're genuinely interested in the other person.

Think about it—how often have you bonded with someone over a shared interest in sports, a mutual love for a TV show, or even a similar frustration with the morning commute? These seemingly trivial conversations help establish common ground, which is the foundation of any strong relationship, personal or professional. And once you've established that connection, the door is open for more meaningful dialogue.

Overcoming the Awkwardness of Small Talk

One of the reasons small talk gets such a bad reputation is because it can feel awkward—especially if you're not sure what to say or if the other person isn't immediately responsive. But here's the thing: small talk, like any other skill, gets easier with practice. The more you engage in it, the more comfortable you'll become, and the more you'll start to see its value.

Start by asking open-ended questions that encourage the other person to share more than just a yes or no answer. For example, instead of asking, "Did you enjoy the event?" you could ask, "What did you think of the keynote speaker's insights on digital transformation?" This not only keeps the conversation flowing but also helps you gather more information that could lead to a deeper discussion.

Another tip is to pay attention to your surroundings and use them as conversation starters. If you're at a conference, comment on the venue, the session you just attended, or the amazing food at the coffee station.

These observations can serve as natural entry points into a conversation, making the interaction feel less forced.

Small Talk in Different Cultures

It's also worth noting that the importance of small talk varies across cultures. In some cultures, like the United States or the United Kingdom, small talk is a crucial part of business and social interactions. In others, such as Germany or Japan, people might prefer to get to the point more quickly. Understanding these cultural nuances can help you tailor your approach and ensure that your small talk is well-received.

For example, in the United States, it's common to start a business meeting with a few minutes of small talk to break the ice. However, in Japan, it's important to be mindful of the fact that small talk may not be as extensive, and getting to the main topic might happen sooner. Being culturally aware not only helps you navigate these interactions more effectively but also shows respect for the other person's preferences and customs.

Embracing the Power of Small Talk

So, the next time you find yourself dismissing small talk as trivial or pointless, remember this: it's not just about the words you exchange—it's about what those words represent. Small talk is a powerful tool for building trust, establishing common ground, and paving the way for deeper, more meaningful conversations. It's the warm-up act that sets the stage for the main event, and without it, you might never get to the conversations that truly matter.

Embrace small talk as an essential part of your networking toolkit. Use it to break the ice, build rapport, and gradually steer the conversation toward the topics that are most important to you. Because at the end of the day, those seemingly small conversations can lead to some pretty big opportunities.

"Courage starts with showing up and letting ourselves be seen."

Brene Brown

CHAPTER 6
THE ART OF NETWORKING

NETWORKING IN DIFFERENT CONTEXTS

In-Person Networking: The Basics

In-person networking is a powerful way to build strong, lasting connections because it allows you to engage with others face-to-face, creating a more personal and memorable interaction. While digital networking has become increasingly popular and effective, in-person networking offers unique opportunities for deeper engagement through direct human interaction. When you meet someone in person, you can read body language, hear tone of voice, and pick up on social cues that are often more subtle in digital environments.

But what exactly does in-person networking entail? At its core, in-person networking involves attending events, gatherings, or meetings where you have the opportunity to meet and interact with people who could potentially contribute to your personal or professional growth. These interactions can take place in various settings, from formal industry conferences and seminars to casual meetups, social events, or even impromptu conversations at a coffee shop.

Why In-Person Networking Matters

In-person networking is highly effective because it allows you to establish trust and rapport quickly. When you meet someone face-to-face, you have the chance to make a strong first impression—something that can be harder to achieve in digital interactions. A firm handshake, direct eye contact, and a warm smile can instantly convey confidence and sincerity, helping to build a connection that is both genuine and lasting.

Moreover, in-person interactions often lead to deeper conversations. Being physically present allows for a more dynamic exchange of ideas, where you can engage in meaningful dialogue, ask thoughtful questions, and share your experiences in a way that feels natural. This level of engagement is crucial for building relationships that go beyond surface-level connections and can lead to valuable collaborations, mentorship opportunities, and long-term partnerships.

Choosing the Right Events

Not all networking events are created equal, and selecting the right ones is key to making the most of your in-person networking efforts. Here are some common types of events where you can network in person:

1. **Industry Conferences and Trade Shows:**

   These events are goldmines for networking within your specific field. Attendees are usually professionals and experts who share your interests and goals, making it easier to find common ground and strike up a conversation. For example, if you work in marketing, attending a digital marketing conference would connect you with peers, potential clients, and industry leaders.

2. **Workshops and Seminars:**

   Smaller and more focused than conferences, workshops and seminars provide a more intimate setting where you can engage with others who are interested in the same topic. The interactive nature of these events also makes it easier to start conversations with fellow attendees, as you'll have shared experiences to discuss.

3. **Networking Mixers and Social Events:**

   These are less formal gatherings, often organized by professional associations, alumni groups, or community organizations. Networking mixers are designed specifically for making connections, so everyone is there for the same reason. These events are great for broadening your network beyond your immediate industry.

4. **Local Meetups and Interest Groups:**

   Don't underestimate the power of local meetups or hobby-based groups. These gatherings bring together people with common interests, and while the focus might not be strictly professional, they offer a relaxed environment to build relationships that could lead to future opportunities.

5. **Volunteering Opportunities:**

   Volunteering is a unique and highly effective way to network in person while giving back to your community. By participating in volunteer activities, you not only contribute to a cause you care about but also connect with like-minded individuals who share your values. Volunteering events often attract people from diverse backgrounds, creating opportunities to meet professionals you might not encounter in your usual circles. Whether you're helping out at a charity event, participating in a community clean-up, or offering your skills to a nonprofit organization, volunteering allows you to build relationships in a collaborative and positive environment while doing good.

6. **Casual Encounters:**

   Networking doesn't have to be confined to structured events. Sometimes, the best connections happen in unexpected places— like while waiting in line for coffee or during a flight. The key is to stay open and approachable, ready to strike up a conversation when the opportunity arises.

How to Prepare for In-Person Networking

Preparation is crucial to making the most of your in-person networking opportunities. Here's how you can get ready:

1. **Set Clear Goals:**

   Before attending an event, think about what you want to achieve. Are you looking to make new connections, learn about industry trends, or find potential collaborators? Having a clear goal in mind will help you stay focused and make the most of your time.

2. **Research Attendees:**

   If possible, find out who will be attending the event. This allows you to identify key people you'd like to meet and even prepare specific questions or topics to discuss with them. LinkedIn is a great tool for researching attendees beforehand.

3. **Prepare Your Elevator Pitch:**

   An elevator pitch is a concise, compelling introduction that explains who you are, what you do, and what makes you unique. Practice your pitch so that you can deliver it confidently when you meet new people.

4. **Share Both Digital and Traditional Business Cards:**

   While digital business cards are becoming the preferred choice at networking events, traditional business cards still hold value in many professional settings. Digital cards, stored conveniently on your phone, allow you to share contact information instantly via QR code or link, making the exchange both seamless and eco-friendly.

On the other hand, traditional business cards offer a tactile, personal touch that some professionals still appreciate. Make sure both your digital and physical cards are updated with your current details, and have them ready for quick access. This balanced approach ensures you're prepared for any situation, leaving either a tech-savvy or classic impression, depending on your audience.

5. **Dress Appropriately:**

First impressions matter, so dress in a way that is appropriate for the event and aligns with your personal brand. Whether it's business casual or formal attire, make sure you feel comfortable and confident in what you're wearing.

Strategies for Successful In-Person Networking

Once you're at the event, it's time to put your preparation into action. Here are some strategies to help you navigate in-person networking effectively:

1. **Arrive Early:**

Arriving early gives you a chance to get comfortable with the setting and start conversations in a more relaxed atmosphere before the event gets crowded. It also shows that you're punctual and serious about networking.

2. **Approach with Confidence:**

Approach new people with confidence, introduce yourself with a smile, and offer a firm handshake. Remember, most people are open to meeting new contacts, so don't be afraid to start a conversation.

3. **Engage in Active Listening:**

   Networking isn't just about talking; it's also about listening. Show genuine interest in what the other person has to say by asking follow-up questions and responding thoughtfully. This builds rapport and makes the conversation more meaningful.

4. **Look for Common Ground:**

   Finding common ground helps to establish a connection quickly. Whether it's a shared interest, a mutual acquaintance, or a similar career path, use these commonalities to deepen the conversation.

5. **Know When to Move On:**

   It's important to balance quality with quantity in networking. While it's great to have in-depth conversations, you also want to meet a variety of people. If the conversation is winding down, politely excuse yourself and move on to meet others.

6. **Follow Up After the Event:**

   The real power of networking lies in the follow-up. After the event, reach out to the people you met with a personalized message. Mention something specific from your conversation to jog their memory and suggest a way to stay in touch, whether it's through LinkedIn or a future coffee meeting.

Maximizing Your In-Person Networking

In-person networking is an invaluable skill that, when done right, can open doors to countless opportunities. By selecting the right events, preparing thoroughly, and engaging confidently, you can build strong, lasting connections that will benefit you both personally and professionally. Remember, networking is not just about what you can gain, but also about what you can give—so approach each interaction with generosity, curiosity, and a genuine interest in others.

INTERACTIVE ELEMENT: EVENT SELECTION AND PREPARATION CHECKLIST

Use this quick checklist to ensure you're selecting the right networking events and preparing effectively:

1. Select the Right Event

☐ Is the event relevant to your industry or interests?

☐ Are key people or companies you want to connect with attending?

☐ Does the event offer opportunities for meaningful conversations (e.g., workshops, small groups)?

2. Do Your Research:

☐ Have you reviewed the attendee list or speakers?

☐ Who are the event sponsors? Sponsors often attract key people from their network, presenting valuable opportunities to meet influential attendees.

☐ Have you identified specific people you want to meet?

☐ Do you have a basic understanding of their work or projects?

3. Prepare Your Introduction:

☐ Have you crafted a brief introduction or elevator pitch?

☐ Do you have a few open-ended questions ready to spark conversation?

☐ Are your business cards or digital contact info (LinkedIn, digital business card, etc.) ready to go?

4. Plan Your Arrival:

☐ Have you planned to arrive early to ease into the event?

☐ Have you set goals for the event (e.g., meet three new contacts)?

☐ Do you have a follow-up plan in mind for after the event?

This checklist will help you select the best events and prepare to make a strong, lasting impression.

ONLINE NETWORKING: THE NEW FRONTIER

Networking isn't limited to conference rooms and coffee shops anymore. In today's digital age, the landscape of networking has expanded dramatically, allowing you to connect with professionals across the globe from the comfort of your own home. Platforms like LinkedIn, X (formerly known as Twitter), and even Instagram have become powerful tools for building professional connections, making it possible to network anytime, anywhere. But to truly stand out in this vast digital space, it's essential to follow best practices that showcase your strengths and make it easy for others to connect with you.

What is Online Networking?

Online networking is the practice of building and maintaining professional relationships through digital platforms. Unlike in-person networking, which relies on face-to-face interactions, online networking uses social media sites, professional networks, and other online communities to connect with peers, mentors, industry leaders, and potential employers or clients. This type of networking is particularly beneficial because it allows you to reach a much broader audience, including people who may not be accessible through traditional networking methods.

Why Online Networking Matters

In today's interconnected world, online networking is more important than ever. It offers a level of convenience and accessibility that in-person networking cannot always match. For instance, if you're unable to attend an industry conference due to geographical or time constraints, online platforms like LinkedIn provide a way to engage with industry professionals, participate in discussions, and stay updated on the latest trends—all without leaving your workplace–or home.

Online networking also allows for continuous engagement. Unlike in-person events, which are typically time-bound, online networking is ongoing. You can connect with someone on LinkedIn, exchange messages, and engage with their content over weeks or months, gradually building a relationship. This ongoing interaction helps to keep you on their radar, making it easier to foster and maintain professional relationships over time.

Getting Started with Online Networking

For those new to online networking, the first step is to establish a strong online presence. Here's how to get started:

1. **Choose the Right Platforms:**

   There are several platforms available for online networking, each with its own strengths. LinkedIn is the most popular platform for professional networking, allowing you to connect with colleagues, join industry groups, and showcase your professional accomplishments. X is another valuable platform, especially for staying updated on industry news and engaging in discussions. Depending on your industry, platforms like Instagram or Facebook might also be relevant, particularly for those in creative fields or small business owners looking to connect with local communities.

2. **Create a Standout Profile:**

   Your online profile is your digital business card, and it's often the first impression others will have of you. On LinkedIn, for example, your profile should be complete, professional, and reflective of your personal brand. Start with a professional photo that presents you in a positive light—studies show that profiles with photos are much more likely to be viewed. Your headline should be more than just your job title; it should convey your value proposition. Instead of "Marketing Manager," consider something like, "Helping Brands Drive Engagement Through Innovative Marketing Strategies." Your summary should be concise and compelling, highlighting your key achievements, skills, and what you bring to the table.

3. **Build and Curate Your Network:**

Once your profile is set up, start building your network. Begin by connecting with people you already know—colleagues, classmates, mentors, and industry peers. From there, expand your network by reaching out to people in your field, joining industry groups, and participating in discussions. When sending connection requests, always personalize your message to explain why you'd like to connect. This not only increases the likelihood of acceptance but also starts the relationship on a positive note.

4. **Engage with Your Network:**

Online networking isn't just about making connections; it's about engaging with them. Regularly update your status with relevant content, such as articles, insights, or news related to your industry. Engage with others by liking, sharing, and commenting on their posts—thoughtful comments can spark deeper conversations and build rapport. Joining LinkedIn groups related to your industry or interests is another great way to connect with like-minded professionals and participate in discussions that can boost your visibility.

Best Practices for Online Networking

To stand out in the digital networking space, it's important to follow best practices that enhance your online presence and foster meaningful connections:

1. Be Consistent:

Consistency is key in online networking. Regularly engage with your network by sharing updates, posting content, and participating in discussions. Consistency not only keeps you visible but also reinforces your commitment to your professional growth and your field.

2. Be Authentic:

Authenticity is just as important online as it is in person. Be genuine in your interactions—whether you're sharing a post, commenting on someone's update, or sending a message. People are more likely to engage with and remember someone who is sincere and true to themselves.

3. Provide Value:

One of the most effective ways to build your online network is by providing value to others. Share insights, offer help, and contribute to discussions in meaningful ways. For example, if someone posts a question related to your expertise, take the time to provide a thoughtful answer. By consistently adding value, you establish yourself as a knowledgeable and helpful resource in your industry.

4. Personalize Your Interactions:

When connecting with new people, avoid sending generic messages. Personalize your connection requests by mentioning something specific about the person's profile, such as a shared interest or a mutual connection. This shows that you've taken the time to learn about them and are genuinely interested in connecting.

5. Follow Up and Maintain Relationships:

Just like in-person networking, the follow-up is crucial in online networking. After connecting with someone, send a thank-you message or engage with their content to keep the relationship warm.

Over time, maintain the connection by checking in periodically, sharing relevant resources, or simply catching up on their latest updates.

6. **Showcase Your Work:**

Many online platforms allow you to showcase your work, whether through a portfolio, articles, or project updates. Use these features to highlight your achievements and demonstrate your expertise. For example, LinkedIn allows you to publish articles or share case studies, which can help position you as a thought leader in your field.

If you're wondering what exactly a thought leader is—it's someone recognized for their expertise in a specific field and whose opinions are sought after. They lead discussions, shape trends, and inspire others to follow their lead. Essentially, they're the trusted voice people listen to.

Challenges of Online Networking

While online networking offers numerous advantages, it also comes with its own set of challenges. For one, it can sometimes feel impersonal, as you miss out on the nuances of face-to-face interactions, like body language and tone. To counter this, try to make your digital interactions as personal as possible by using video calls for more important conversations and being mindful of your tone in written communications.

Another challenge is managing the sheer volume of information and connections that online networking can generate. It's easy to get overwhelmed by the constant flow of updates, messages, and notifications. To manage this, set aside specific times for networking activities and be selective about which connections and groups you engage with regularly.

Maximizing Your Online Networking

Online networking has become an essential tool in the modern professional landscape, offering a way to build and maintain connections that transcend geographical boundaries. By establishing a strong online presence, engaging consistently and authentically, and providing value to your network, you can effectively navigate the digital networking space and unlock new opportunities for growth and collaboration. Remember, online networking is a marathon, not a sprint—so be patient, stay committed, and watch your network flourish over time.

Leveraging Online Networking for a Career Transition

Online networking, when done strategically, can help you build connections, showcase your expertise, and gain visibility in your target industry. It's not just about sending out connection requests—it's about positioning yourself as a knowledgeable and engaged professional who's ready to bring value to a new field. Let's explore how one professional, Lisa, used LinkedIn to navigate a significant career shift, moving from the world of marketing to the tech industry, all by leveraging the power of online networking.

Lisa had always been a powerhouse in the marketing world, known for her creative campaigns and knack for turning consumer insights into blockbuster products. But after a decade of rising through the ranks, she began to feel a familiar itch—the kind that signals it's time for a change. The problem was, the change she wanted wasn't a simple one. Lisa wasn't just looking for a new job; she was aiming for a new industry entirely. The tech world had always fascinated her, but breaking into it felt like trying to board a moving train.

Undeterred by the challenge, Lisa decided to take a strategic, digital-first approach to her career pivot. She knew that in today's professional landscape, LinkedIn wasn't just a platform—it was the place where careers were made, especially when you were venturing into uncharted territory.

Lisa began by giving her LinkedIn profile a complete makeover. She didn't just tweak her job titles; she reimagined her professional identity. Her headline boldly announced her intent: "Marketing Strategist Transitioning to Tech I Passionate About AI & Digital Transformation." Her summary highlighted her strengths in data-driven marketing, digital innovation, and the ways these skills could apply to the tech industry. She carefully crafted her profile to reflect not only where she had been but also where she wanted to go.

Next, Lisa set out to immerse herself in the tech community, but she wasn't about to be a passive observer. She started by curating a stream of industry-relevant content—everything from articles on AI and machine learning to deep dives into the latest digital marketing trends in tech. Each post was an opportunity to share her insights and start conversations. She wasn't just posting links; she was adding value, offering her perspective on why these trends mattered and how they intersected with her marketing expertise.

But Lisa knew that content alone wouldn't be enough. She needed to engage with the standout figures in the tech world. So, she began actively commenting on posts from tech leaders and influencers, not with generic praise, but with thoughtful, well-researched responses that reflected her unique blend of marketing savvy and emerging tech knowledge. Slowly but surely, her name started to pop up in the notifications of industry heavyweights.

Then came the moment that would change everything. After posting a particularly insightful comment on a discussion about AI-driven consumer insights, Lisa noticed a new connection request. It was from a senior executive at a leading tech firm—a leader in the industry. The accompanying message was personal and direct: he appreciated her perspective and wanted to hear more about her views on the convergence of marketing and technology.

This initial message led to a series of conversations, where Lisa and the executive discussed everything from market trends to career transitions. He was impressed by her proactive approach and the depth of her insights, and before long, he offered to mentor her through her career shift. This relationship became a cornerstone of Lisa's transition into the tech world. The executive introduced her to key players in the industry, provided insider advice, and even helped her navigate potential job opportunities.

What started as a simple decision to leverage LinkedIn more effectively had evolved into a powerful network of support. With her mentor's guidance and the connections she had cultivated, Lisa was able to land interviews with tech companies that previously seemed out of reach. Before long, she secured a marketing role at a tech startup, where she could apply her skills in a whole new arena.

Lisa's story is a perfect example of how online networking, when done strategically, can open doors to entirely new industries. By consistently sharing relevant content, engaging thoughtfully with leaders, and reaching out with personalized connection requests, she didn't just transition into a new career—she built a network that set her up for success in a completely different field.

"The currency of real networking is not greed but generosity."

Keith Ferrazzi

CHAPTER 7

BUILDING AND MAINTAINING YOUR NETWORK

FOLLOWING UP: THE KEY TO LASTING CONNECTIONS

Building a network is just the beginning—keeping it alive and thriving is where the real effort comes in. You've attended the events, exchanged business cards, or connected online. But what happens next? If you think the job is done, think again. The true power of networking lies not in the initial meeting but in the follow-up. It's the follow-up that transforms brief encounters into meaningful, lasting connections.

But let's be honest, a generic "nice to meet you" won't leave much of an impression. You know the kind—the kind of email or message that's so bland and forgettable it could have been sent by a bot. To truly stand out, you need to invest the time. Building and maintaining relationships doesn't happen overnight—it requires consistent effort and dedication.

Your follow-up needs to be thoughtful, timely, and personalized. This is your chance to show that you're serious about building a relationship, not just collecting contacts.

Why Following Up Matters

Following up is more than just a polite gesture; it's a crucial step in the networking process. Think of it as watering a plant after you've planted the seed. Without that water (your follow-up), the seed (your initial connection) may never grow into anything substantial. A well-executed follow-up shows that you value the connection, that you're proactive, and that you're genuinely interested in maintaining the relationship.

In the world of networking, the people who follow up are the ones who stay top of mind. Whether you're following up after a networking event, a business meeting, or even a brief chat at a coffee shop, the goal is to reinforce the connection and keep the conversation going. It's about moving from "nice to meet you" to "let's work together" or "let's keep in touch." Essentially, following up turns a potential opportunity into a real one.

Getting Started with Following Up

If you're new to the concept of following up, don't worry—it's simpler than it might seem. Here's how to get started:

1. **Be Timely:**

   Timing is everything in the world of follow-ups. You don't want to wait so long that the person forgets who you are, but you also don't want to come across as overly eager. A good rule of thumb is to follow up within 24 to 48 hours after your initial interaction. This shows that you're interested and organized without being pushy. If you're reaching out after a meeting, this timing allows you to catch the person while the conversation is still fresh in their mind.

2. **Personalize Your Message:**

The quickest way to make your follow-up stand out is by making it personal. Instead of a generic "nice to meet you," reference something specific from your conversation. Did you discuss a particular project, shared interest, or mutual acquaintance? Mention it. Personalization shows that you were truly engaged during your interaction and that you're not just sending the same message to everyone. For example, "I really enjoyed our conversation about the challenges of digital marketing in the nonprofit sector. Your insights were invaluable, and I'd love to continue our discussion."

3. **Offer Value:**

A great way to make your follow-up memorable is by offering something of value. This could be a helpful resource, an introduction to someone in your network, or even just a relevant article or book recommendation. The idea is to show that you're not just looking to get something from the relationship but that you're also willing to give. For instance, "Based on our conversation about expanding into new markets, I thought you might find this article on global marketing strategies useful."

4. **Include a Call to Action:**

Your follow-up should also include a clear call to action—something that keeps the momentum going. This could be an invitation to meet again, a request for their thoughts on a specific topic, or a suggestion for how you might collaborate. The key is to make it easy for the other person to continue the conversation. For example, "I'd love to grab coffee next week to discuss how we might collaborate on the upcoming project. Let me know what time works best for you."

5. **Be Genuine and Gracious:**

Above all, your follow-up should be genuine. Express your appreciation for the person's time and insights, and let them know you're looking forward to staying in touch. A little gratitude goes a long way in building strong, lasting relationships. "Thank you again for taking the time to chat with me at the conference. I really appreciated your advice on leadership development, and I'm excited to apply it in my role."

BEST PRACTICES FOR EFFECTIVE FOLLOW-UPS

To truly master the art of following up, it's important to adhere to some best practices that will help you maintain your network and keep relationships strong:

1. **Be Consistent:**

Follow-ups shouldn't just happen after the first meeting. Consistency is key to maintaining your network. Check in periodically—whether it's every few weeks or months—to keep the relationship warm. This could be as simple as sending a holiday greeting, congratulating them on a recent achievement, or sharing a piece of news that might interest them.

2. **Tailor Your Approach:**

Different situations call for different follow-up strategies. A follow-up after a casual networking event might be more informal, while a follow-up after a formal business meeting should be more structured. Tailor your approach to fit the context and the nature of the relationship.

3. Don't Overdo It:

While it's important to stay in touch, you don't want to overwhelm the other person with too many messages. Strike a balance between being persistent and being respectful of their time. If you don't hear back after your initial follow-up, it's okay to send a gentle reminder after a week or two, but don't push too hard.

4. Use Different Channels:

Depending on your relationship, consider mixing up your follow-up methods. An email might be appropriate for a business contact, while a LinkedIn message or even a handwritten note could stand out more for someone you've built a closer rapport with. The key is to choose the channel that best suits the relationship and the context of your follow-up.

5. Track Your Interactions:

Keeping a record of your follow-up interactions is crucial for staying organized and ensuring you don't let important connections slip through the cracks. Tools like a CRM system—such as Zoho, Creatio.com, Hubspot, FreshShales and others—can help you track when you last connected with someone, what you discussed, and when it's time to follow up again. The right CRM depends on your business size and budget. Keep in mind your company may already have one in place.

Examples of Effective Follow-Ups

To bring these ideas to life, here are some examples of effective follow-ups tailored to different scenarios:

- **After a Networking Event:**

  "Hi [Name], it was great meeting you at the industry mixer last night. I really enjoyed our conversation about the latest trends in data analytics. If you're open to it, I'd love to grab coffee sometime next week to dive deeper into the topic and discuss potential collaboration opportunities. Looking forward to hearing from you!"

- **After a Business Meeting:**

  "Dear [Name], thank you for the productive meeting this morning. I appreciate the opportunity to discuss how we can work together on the new project. I've attached the documents we discussed, and I'm excited to move forward with the next steps. Please let me know if you need any further information, and I look forward to our continued collaboration."

- **Reconnecting with an Old Contact:**

  "Hi [Name], it's been a while since we last caught up! I've been following your work and was really impressed by your recent achievements in sustainable design. I'd love to reconnect and hear more about what you've been up to—how does lunch next Tuesday or Thursday sound? If those dates don't work, I'm flexible and happy to find a time that suits you!"

- **After Receiving Help or Advice:**

  "Hi [Name], I wanted to take a moment to thank you again for your invaluable advice during our conversation last week. Your insights on market entry strategies have given me a lot to think about, and I'm already working on implementing your suggestions. I really appreciate your support and would love to stay in touch as I continue to navigate this project."

The Power of a Thoughtful Follow-Up

Following up is the bridge that turns initial connections into meaningful relationships. It's the extra step that shows you're serious about maintaining and growing your network. By being timely, personalized, and value-driven in your follow-ups, you can ensure that your connections don't just stay on the surface but grow into something substantial and mutually beneficial.

Remember, it's not just about making a good first impression—it's about keeping that impression alive and well in the minds of the people you meet. So, the next time you make a new connection, don't just let it sit there—nurture it with a thoughtful follow-up and watch it flourish.

ADDING VALUE: THE SECRET TO STRONGER CONNECTIONS

So, you've made a connection and followed up—great! But what now? How do you ensure that this relationship doesn't just fizzle out but instead grows into something meaningful and lasting? The answer lies in adding value. This concept might sound a bit abstract at first, but it's actually one of the most straightforward and effective ways to solidify your place in someone's network. And here's the best part: adding value is all about giving, not taking.

My Network: Stories and Lessons:

A few years ago, I was working on a project that required insights into a niche market I wasn't very familiar with—a market that could make or break the success of our new product launch. Feeling a bit out of my depth, I decided to reach out to an old colleague, Gwen, who had built her career around this very industry. I hadn't spoken to Gwen in a while, but I remembered how knowledgeable she was and hoped she might be willing to share some of her expertise.

When I called Gwen, I was upfront about needing her help, and to my relief, she was more than willing to chat. We spent nearly an hour on the phone, during which I asked a lot of questions, scribbled down notes as fast as I could, and absorbed everything she shared. Gwen was generous with her insights, providing me with a much clearer understanding of the market landscape and even suggesting some strategies I hadn't considered.

After the call, I felt incredibly grateful for the time she took to help me. I wanted to show my appreciation in a way that went beyond just saying "thank you," so I decided to send her a handwritten note along with a couple of articles and a book I'd recently read that I thought might be relevant to her work. I remember carefully choosing the articles, making sure they were insightful and aligned with the challenges she had mentioned she was facing in her own projects. I didn't expect anything in return—I simply wanted to acknowledge her kindness and hopefully provide something of value in return.

To my surprise, a few weeks later, I received an email from Gwen. Not only did she thank me for the thoughtful note and resources, but she also mentioned that she had a colleague, Mark, who was looking for someone with my specific skill set to consult on a major project. She thought we would be a great match and offered to introduce us.

That introduction led to a significant opportunity—one that turned out to be a pivotal moment in my company. Working with Mark led to collaborations that expanded my network and expertise in ways I couldn't have imagined.

Reflecting on that experience, I realized just how powerful adding value can be in building and maintaining professional relationships. By taking the time to show genuine appreciation and offer something meaningful, I wasn't just thanking Gwen—I was strengthening a connection that ultimately gave back in ways I hadn't anticipated. It taught me that when you consistently look for ways to help others, without expecting anything in return, you build a network that's not just supportive, but eager to help you succeed when the right opportunity arises.

What Does It Mean to Add Value?

Adding value means offering something of genuine benefit to your connections without expecting anything in return. It's about being proactive in finding ways to support, help, or enrich the lives of those in your network. This could be through sharing knowledge, offering your expertise, providing opportunities, or even just lending a listening ear when someone needs it. The idea is to be the kind of person who others see as a valuable resource—someone they can turn to not just when they need something, but when they want to collaborate, brainstorm, or share ideas.

Think of it this way: in any relationship, whether personal or professional, the strongest bonds are built on mutual trust and support. By consistently adding value to your connections, you show that you're invested in their success and well-being, which naturally builds trust. Over time, this positions you as a go-to person in your network, someone who others want to stay connected with because they know that you bring something valuable to the table.

Why Adding Value Matters

In the world of networking, it's easy to focus on what you can gain—new opportunities, career advancement, collaborations. But the most successful networkers know that the real magic happens when you shift the focus to what you can give. Adding value isn't just a nice thing to do; it's a powerful strategy for building long-term, meaningful relationships. When you offer value without expecting anything in return, you create goodwill. People remember those who helped them, especially when that help was unsolicited and genuinely useful.

Moreover, adding value links directly to your follow-up strategy. After you've made that initial connection, following up is the first step in staying on someone's radar. But to keep that relationship warm and thriving, you need to continue showing up in a way that benefits the other person. This is where adding value comes in. It's the follow-up after the follow-up—the way you keep the momentum going and ensure that the connection doesn't stagnate.

How to Start Adding Value

If you're new to the idea of adding value, don't worry—it's easier than you might think. Here's how you can get started:

1. **Share Knowledge:**

   One of the simplest ways to add value is by sharing knowledge. This could be an article, a book recommendation, or even a piece of advice that you think might be useful to someone in your network. The key is to make it relevant and tailored to the person's interests or needs. For example, if you know someone is struggling with a particular business challenge, sending them a link to a helpful resource can show that you're thinking of them and their success.

2. Make Introductions:

Sometimes, the best way to add value is by connecting people within your network. If you know two people who could benefit from knowing each other—whether because of shared interests, complementary skills, or potential collaboration—make an introduction. This not only helps both parties but also positions you as a connector, someone who brings people together. For example, "I'd like to introduce you to [Name]. I think you both could benefit from each other's expertise in [specific area]."

3. Offer Your Expertise:

If you have a particular skill or area of expertise, offer it to those in your network. This could be anything from reviewing a project proposal to providing strategic advice on a challenge they're facing. The idea is to be generous with your knowledge and skills, offering them in a way that genuinely helps others. For instance, "If you need a second pair of eyes on your presentation, I'd be happy to take a look."

4. Support Their Work:

Another way to add value is by supporting the work of those in your network. This could be as simple as liking, sharing, or commenting on their content on social media, attending an event they're hosting, or even spreading the word about their business. Publicly supporting someone's work not only helps them but also shows that you're invested in their success. For example, "I shared your latest blog post with my team—it had some great insights we're going to apply in our strategy."

5. Provide Constructive Feedback:

If someone in your network shares a project or idea with you and asks for your input, offering constructive feedback can be incredibly valuable. The key is to be supportive while providing actionable advice that can help them improve. This kind of feedback is often appreciated because it shows that you care enough to think critically about their work. For instance, "I really liked your approach in the proposal. One suggestion I have is to add more data to support your key points—it could make an even stronger case."

BEST PRACTICES FOR ADDING VALUE

To truly make adding value a part of your networking strategy, it's important to follow some best practices:

1. **Be Genuine:**

   The value you offer should come from a place of genuine interest and care. People can sense when you're being sincere versus when you're just trying to curry favor. Always look for ways to add value that align with your strengths and interests, and that genuinely benefit the other person.

2. **Be Consistent:**

   Adding value shouldn't be a one-time thing. Make it a regular part of how you interact with your network. Whether it's sharing useful resources, offering help, or checking in to see how someone is doing, consistency is key to building strong relationships.

3. **Tailor Your Approach:**

   Not everyone in your network will need the same kind of value. Tailor your approach based on the individual's needs, interests, and the nature of your relationship. What's valuable to one person might not be to another, so it's important to personalize your efforts.

4. **Don't Expect Anything in Return:**

The whole point of adding value is to give without expecting anything in return. While it's natural to hope that your generosity will lead to reciprocal actions, it's important not to let this become your primary motivation. When you add value selflessly, the benefits often come back to you in unexpected ways.

5. **Follow Up with Value:**

Remember, adding value is a great way to keep the connection alive after your initial follow-up. For example, if you've recently connected with someone at an event and followed up with a thank-you email, your next step could be to send them a useful article or offer help with a project they mentioned. This keeps the relationship moving forward and shows that you're serious about staying connected.

Examples of Adding Value

Here are some examples of how you can add value in different networking situations:

- **After a Networking Event:**

"Hi [Name], it was great meeting you at the conference. I really enjoyed our conversation about sustainable business practices. I came across this article on green supply chain management and thought you might find it useful. Looking forward to staying in touch!"

- **When Someone Shares a Project:**

"Hi [Name], thank you for sharing your new project with me. I really like the direction you're taking. One suggestion I have is to consider adding a case study to highlight your success in a similar project—it could really strengthen your proposal."

- **Offering an Introduction:**

  "Hi [Name], I'd like to introduce you to [Name]. She's an expert in digital marketing, and I think her insights could be really valuable as you expand your online presence. I've cc'd her on this email so you can connect directly."

- **Supporting Their Work:**

  "Hi [Name], I just saw your latest article on LinkedIn—great work! I shared it with a few colleagues who I know are interested in the topic. Keep up the fantastic work, and let me know if there's anything I can do to support your efforts."

The Power of Adding Value

Adding value is one of the most powerful ways to strengthen your professional network. It's about being a giver, not just a taker, and building relationships based on trust, support, and mutual success. By consistently offering value to your connections, you not only solidify your place in their network but also position yourself as a reliable and resourceful person they can count on. So, the next time you're thinking about how to maintain a connection, ask yourself: "How can I add value to this person's life or work?" The answer might just be the key to building a lasting, meaningful relationship.

"Surround yourself with people who are smarter than you. Pick people who are interested in what you're interested in, and who will help you think outside the box. "

Lynn Tilton

CHAPTER 8

ADVANCED NETWORKING STRATEGIES

By now, you've likely developed a strong foundation in networking. You know the basics—how to introduce yourself, make a solid first impression, and maintain professional connections. But what happens after you've built your initial network? How do you expand and deepen those connections to unlock even more opportunities?

And don't worry, the word "advanced" shouldn't feel intimidating. Think of this as the next step in a process you're already familiar with—a natural evolution in your networking journey. Advanced networking isn't about doing more; it's about being more intentional, strategic, and thoughtful in how you approach and build relationships over time.

BUILDING A NETWORK OF INFLUENCE

As you continue to level up your networking game, one of the most powerful outcomes is creating what's known as a *network of influence*. This goes beyond simply knowing a lot of people or collecting business cards—it's about surrounding yourself with individuals who are well-respected, connected, and influential in your industry. These are the key players who can not only open doors for you but also trust your abilities enough to recommend you, collaborate with you, or seek you out when opportunities arise.

So, What Exactly is a "Network of Influence"?

Think of a network of influence like a VIP list of your industry. It's made up of people whose opinions matter, whose names carry weight, and who can make things happen with a few phone calls or emails. In a network of influence, there's a mutual respect and trust. These individuals value what you bring to the table, whether it's your expertise, your work ethic, or your innovative ideas. In return, they can offer you advice, connections, and opportunities that might otherwise be out of reach.

Why is a Network of Influence Important?

Imagine you're working on a major project and need feedback from someone with deep industry knowledge. Or perhaps you're eyeing a new job opportunity but need a referral from a trusted source. This is where your network of influence comes into play. These are the people who can vouch for you, offer insights based on years of experience, and guide you toward success because they *know* you and respect your work.

A strong network of influence isn't just about having access to opportunities—it's about being part of a trusted circle where everyone supports each other's growth and success.

Building Trust First

Let's get one thing clear: trust is the foundation. You can't build a network of influence by being transactional or self-serving. People value authenticity, reliability, and consistency. To be welcomed into their circles, you need to show that you're someone they can rely on—whether it's for delivering results, offering support, or simply keeping your word.

Steps to Build Your Own Network of Influence

1. **Find Your Industry's Power Players** Start by pinpointing the people who are key players in your industry. These are the leaders, innovators, and influencers who not only have deep experience but also command respect. They might be the ones regularly invited to speak at conferences, leading major projects, or making waves through thought leadership on platforms like LinkedIn or X.

   But don't just look at their titles—pay attention to their reputation, their body of work, and how they engage with others. These are the people who set the trends and lead the conversation in your field.

2. **Offer More Than You Take** Once you've identified key players, the next step is figuring out how to add value to them. You can't just walk up to someone influential and say, "How can I help you?" Instead, take the time to learn about their work, their challenges, and their goals. Then, find ways to support them in a way that aligns with your strengths.

   Maybe you share an insightful article with them, offer feedback on something they've posted, or introduce them to someone in your network who could help solve a problem. The goal is to build a relationship where they see you as a helpful, trustworthy person—not someone just trying to gain favors.

3. **Listen, Learn, and Contribute** Networking with influential people requires a more thoughtful approach. You're not just looking to have a casual conversation—you're aiming to make a meaningful connection. Engage with them by commenting on their work, asking

thoughtful questions, or contributing to discussions they're part of. But be careful not to overdo it. Be respectful of people's time. People are often busy, so don't flood their inbox with messages or try to force a connection. It's about quality over quantity. Engage authentically and allow the relationship to grow over time.

4. **Cultivate Long-Term Relationships** Remember, a network of influence isn't built overnight. Just like any strong relationship, it takes time, effort, and consistent engagement. Check in periodically, offer support when appropriate, and stay connected. Over time, as you build trust and rapport, these influential individuals will start to see you as part of their trusted circle.

5. **Be Seen as a Thought Leader** To truly cement your place in a network of influence, you need to demonstrate that you're not just another professional—you're someone with valuable insights and expertise. Share your own knowledge by writing articles, speaking at events, or even just contributing thoughtful insights to conversations in your field. When influential people see that you have something meaningful to contribute, they'll be more likely to view you as a peer and engage with you at a deeper level.

Advanced Networking Doesn't Have to Be Tedious

At this point, you might be thinking, "This sounds like a lot of work." But here's the good news: advanced networking doesn't have to feel tedious. It's all about working smarter, not harder. When you approach networking with the right mindset—one of curiosity, collaboration, and giving—the process feels less like a chore and more like a natural part of your professional life.

The key is to integrate networking into your routine and build on your foundation, so it becomes something you do regularly, without it feeling forced. You can build these connections at industry events, on LinkedIn, through email, or even during informal interactions like coffee chats. The more you practice, the easier it becomes, and the stronger your network grows.

Personal Story: How I Built a Relationship with an Industry Influencer

I'll be the first to admit—when I first started networking with influential figures in my industry, I didn't have it all figured out. It was one of those trial-by-fire situations where I just hoped I wouldn't make a complete fool of myself. I remember attending a major industry event where one of the key speakers was a well-known figure in my field—let's call her Jane. Jane had the kind of authority and influence that I knew could be a game-changer for my career, but the idea of approaching her? Intimidating, to say the least.

Still, I knew that if I didn't take the opportunity to connect with her, I'd regret it. So, I paid close attention to her speech and picked up on a few key themes she was passionate about. This turned out to be more useful than I realized at the time.

After the event, I didn't rush over to her, like everyone else did. I took a different approach. I waited for a moment when the crowd had thinned out, and I could approach her in a more relaxed setting. When I finally did, instead of jumping straight into how much I admired her work or (even worse) talking about myself, I started by complimenting a specific point from her presentation that I genuinely connected with. I asked a thoughtful question related to her ideas, showing that I wasn't just there to take, but also to learn. To my surprise, Jane lit up. She loved talking about her work, and by showing genuine curiosity, I had made the conversation about her insights, not about me or what I wanted.

From there, the conversation flowed naturally. I didn't rush to get to the point or try to pitch myself—something I know I would've done in my earlier networking attempts. Instead, I asked about the projects she was working on, offering some of my own thoughts where it made sense. And here's what really worked: I followed up by sending a thoughtful email the next day, referencing that conversation and offering a useful resource I thought she'd appreciate.

What I noticed? When you approach influencers with curiosity, listen to what they have to say, and engage them without expecting something immediately in return, it leaves a lasting impression. Jane and I didn't become instant best friends, but we maintained a connection. Over time, that relationship evolved, and she eventually became one of my key mentors—someone I could turn to for advice, introductions, and even collaborations.

Step-by-Step Guide to Approaching and Engaging Influencers

Building relationships with key influencers can significantly elevate your network and open doors to valuable opportunities. However, engaging influencers—whether they're industry leaders, thought leaders, or highly respected professionals—requires a thoughtful approach. Here's a step-by-step guide to help you build meaningful connections with influencers, without coming off as transactional or insincere.

1. **Research Thoroughly**

    Before reaching out to an influencer, make sure you know who they are, what they care about, and what they're currently working on. This groundwork is crucial because it shows that you respect their time and are genuinely interested in their work, not just their influence.

How to do it:

- Follow them on social media (LinkedIn, Twitter, Instagram, etc.).

- Read articles they've written or listen to interviews they've given.

- Study the projects or companies they are associated with.

  This research will not only help you understand what topics or themes resonate with them but also give you conversation starters.

2. Become a Thoughtful Participant, Not a Passive Follower

It's easy to follow someone on X (formerly Twitter) or LinkedIn, but true engagement starts when you contribute meaningful insights. Influencers are inundated with likes and comments, so standing out means bringing something fresh to the table.

How to do it:

- Don't just like their post—challenge or expand on their ideas with a well-researched response. Offer a unique perspective, even if it's a respectful disagreement, to get noticed as someone with critical thinking.

- Start discussions in the comments section or share your own personal experience related to their content. For example, if an influencer talks about leadership challenges, share a brief but insightful experience of how you overcame a leadership hurdle. Relatability is powerful.

- Use threads on X or LinkedIn to dive deeper into their key talking points, presenting your take on it with original research or data. Tag them when appropriate.

- This turns you from a passive follower into an active participant in their world, making you more memorable.

3. Add Value Before Asking for Anything

One of the biggest mistakes people make when reaching out to influencers is immediately asking for something—advice, an introduction, a partnership. Before you ask for anything, focus on adding value to their work or goals. This might involve sharing a resource, connecting them to someone who could help them, or offering to assist on a project.

How to do it:

- Share an article or resource you think might be useful to them.

- If you're in a position to help, offer your expertise on a project they're working on.

- Introduce them to someone in your network who can add value to their current work or goals.

  This demonstrates that you're not just looking for what you can gain but are genuinely invested in their success.

4. Make a Personal, Genuine Introduction

When you do reach out, keep your message brief, respectful, and personalized. Explain how their work has impacted you, and offer a reason why you'd like to connect. Be specific about why their insights or collaboration would be valuable to you, and ensure it doesn't come off as purely self-serving.

How to do it:

- Keep the message short—two or three sentences max.

- Mention something specific about their work that resonated with you.

- Offer a sincere compliment and provide a clear reason for why you'd like to connect, without immediately asking for too much.

Example: *"Hi [Name], I've been following your work on sustainable business practices, and I found your recent podcast on supply chain innovation incredibly insightful. I'd love to connect and learn more about how you approach industry disruptions—your expertise is something I really admire. Thank you for your time!"*

5. Stay Consistent, but Respectful of Their Time

Once you've connected, don't expect the relationship to blossom overnight. Influencers are busy, and building a relationship takes time. Stay in touch regularly but without overwhelming them.

How to do it:

- Engage with their content periodically by commenting on new articles or updates.

- Check in every few months with a thoughtful message, resource, or idea that aligns with their interests.

- Avoid inundating them with messages or requests. Be patient and allow the relationship to develop naturally.

Your Personalized Influencer Engagement Plan

Ready to build a meaningful connection with an industry influencer? Use this quick step-by-step guide to create your own personalized engagement plan.

1. **Identify an Influencer:**

   Think about someone in your industry whom you admire and respect. In the space below, Write down their name and why you'd like to connect with them. Consider what you've learned from their work or how their ideas have impacted you.

   Name:

   _____

   Why I want to connect:

   _____

2. **Do Your Research:**

   Find out more about their work. Identify the topics or projects they're passionate about. Below, list three specific things you've discovered about them that you can reference when reaching out.

   _____

   _____

   _____

3. **Engage Authentically:**

   Comment on one of their recent posts on Instagram, LinkedIn or X (formerly Twitter). Make sure to add value by sharing a thoughtful insight or asking a meaningful question. Then, write down how you engaged.

Commented on their recent post about _____ and shared my thoughts on _____.

4. **Plan Your First Message:**

Craft a short, personalized message for when you're ready to reach out. Make it specific and genuine, referencing the research you've done. Keep it to two or three sentences, and avoid asking for anything upfront.

Example: "Hi [Name], I really enjoyed your recent article on [topic]. Your perspective on [specific insight] resonated with me, and I've been applying similar strategies in my work. I'd love to connect and continue learning from your expertise!"

5. **Track Your Progress:**

Note when you've reached out and set a reminder to follow up in a few months if needed. Use this space to track how the relationship develops and any steps you take to stay engaged.

Summary:

In this chapter, the focus shifts to taking your networking efforts to a more strategic and intentional level. It's about moving beyond just meeting people and building connections that can truly influence your career or business. One key aspect is creating a Network of Influence, surrounding yourself with individuals who are respected, well-connected, and trust your abilities. These relationships are invaluable for providing insights, referrals, and opportunities that might otherwise be out of reach.

Engaging with industry influencers requires thoughtful planning and genuine interaction. The chapter outlines how to approach these key figures, from doing your research and engaging meaningfully, to adding value before asking for anything in return. Building these connections takes time, but the rewards are worth the effort.

These advanced networking strategies, when implemented thoughtfully, will deepen your connections, elevate your professional reputation, and open new opportunities for collaboration and growth.

The only true measure of success is the ratio between what we might have done and what we might have been on the one hand, and the thing we have made and the things we have made of ourselves on the other.

H. G. Wells

CHAPTER 9

MEASURING NETWORKING SUCCESS

We've spent a lot of time talking about the importance of networking and how to build strong, lasting connections. But here's a question: How do you know if your networking efforts are actually working? It's easy to collect business cards or grow your LinkedIn connections, but true networking success goes beyond just numbers. It's about measurable, tangible results that contribute to your personal and professional growth.

That's where setting and tracking networking goals come into play. Just like any other business or career objective, your networking efforts need to be strategic and purposeful. And that means setting clear goals and measuring your progress toward them.

Why Setting Networking Goals Is Essential

Let's start with the basics: why should you set goals for networking in the first place?

Without goals, networking can feel like an aimless activity. You might attend events or reach out to people, but if you don't have a clear purpose, it's difficult to gauge whether you're making progress. Networking goals help you stay focused, giving your efforts direction and ensuring that you're not just going through the motions.

Think of networking like a long-term investment. Every conversation, connection, and follow-up is like planting a seed. But how will you know if those seeds are growing into opportunities if you don't track them? By setting specific goals, you can measure the results of your efforts and make adjustments along the way.

Setting Networking Goals

Now that you understand the importance of networking goals, let's dive into how to set them. You want your goals to be SMART—Specific, Measurable, Achievable, Relevant, and Time-bound. This framework will help you create goals that are clear, actionable, and aligned with your overall professional objectives.

Here's how to break it down:

Specific

Your networking goals should be clear and precise. Avoid vague statements like "I want to network more." Instead, specify what you want to achieve, such as, "I want to connect with five new people in my industry each month."

Measurable

You can't improve what you can't measure. Having measurable networking goals ensures that you can evaluate your efforts and make adjustments as needed. Think of it like running a race—you need to know the distance to understand how close you are to the finish line. For instance, instead of vaguely planning to "attend events," set a concrete target like, "I will attend two industry conferences and participate in three webinars this quarter." Tracking progress doesn't just give you a sense of achievement—it helps you stay accountable.

Achievable

It's great to dream big, but when it comes to networking, you need to be practical. If you're new to networking, don't set yourself up for failure by aiming too high. For example, rather than setting a goal of reaching out to 100 people in a month, aim to connect with five key individuals whose work genuinely interests you. Start with small, meaningful steps and build your confidence as you go. It's like lifting weights—you don't start with the heaviest; you work your way up.

Relevant

Your networking efforts should serve your broader career or business goals. Don't waste time attending every event just because it's available—focus on the ones that are directly tied to your objectives. If you're looking to expand into international markets, then your networking goals should revolve around connecting with people who have experience or influence in those areas. For instance, "I want to connect with three professionals who have successfully expanded their business into Europe by the end of this year."

Time-bound

Without deadlines, even the best intentions can fade. Set time-bound goals to keep yourself moving forward and create a sense of urgency. For example, instead of saying "I'll connect with potential mentors," set a clear deadline: "I will have conversations with three potential mentors by the end of this quarter." Deadlines keep you focused and prevent procrastination, turning vague ambitions into concrete, actionable steps.

Examples of Networking Goals

To bring it all together, here are some practical examples of measurable networking goals you can set for yourself:

Attend one networking event per month.

Whether it's an industry conference, a local business meetup, or an online webinar, commit to showing up at one event every month. This ensures you're consistently expanding your network.

Schedule three coffee chats or virtual meetings per quarter.

These one-on-one conversations are invaluable for building deeper connections. Make it a point to set up three of these meetings every quarter, whether in person or virtually.

Follow up with five new contacts within 48 hours of meeting them.

Networking isn't just about the initial meeting—it's about building relationships. Set a goal to follow up with new connections within two days, whether it's via email or LinkedIn.

Seek out one new mentor or advisor each year.

Mentorship can have a huge impact on your career growth. Set a goal to connect with a new mentor each year, someone who can guide you and offer valuable insights into your field.

Engage with your network on LinkedIn once a week.

Networking isn't always about attending events. You can nurture your network online by commenting on posts, sharing valuable content, and congratulating others on their achievements.

Tracking Your Progress

Setting networking goals is only half the battle—you also need a system for tracking your progress. Without tracking, it's hard to see how far you've come and what adjustments you need to make along the way.

Here's how you can track your networking progress:

✓ **Track your Activities** Keep a record of your networking activities in your CRM of choice. Include details like the date, the person you connected with, the method of connection, and any follow-up actions. This will give you a clear overview of your efforts and help you stay organized with your follow-ups.

✓ **Set Reminders** Use your calendar or task management app to set reminders for networking tasks. For instance, if you meet someone at an event, set a reminder to follow up within 48 hours. Or, if you've arranged a coffee chat, schedule a reminder to send a thank-you email afterward.

✓ **Review Your Progress Regularly** Set aside time monthly or quarterly to review your networking progress. Have you achieved the goals you set? If not, reflect on what changes you can make to improve your results next time. This regular review keeps you accountable and ensures you stay on track.

✓ **Celebrate Milestones** Networking requires effort, so it's essential to recognize your achievements. When you reach a milestone—whether it's attending an event, securing a mentor, or expanding your network—celebrate your success. Acknowledging these wins will keep you motivated to continue building your network.

THE BIGGER PICTURE

Remember, networking isn't just about hitting arbitrary targets—it's about building meaningful relationships that support your career or business growth. Setting and tracking measurable goals helps ensure that your efforts are productive and purposeful. But at the end of the day, it's the quality of your connections, not just the quantity, that will define your networking success.

Networking is a long-term investment. The relationships you build today may not pay off immediately, but over time, they can lead to new opportunities, collaborations, and growth. By setting clear goals and tracking your progress, you'll stay motivated, focused, and on the path to networking success.

Evaluating ROI: How to Measure the Return on Your Networking Efforts

Once you've set clear networking goals and have been actively tracking your progress, it's time to go a step further—evaluating the *return on investment (ROI)* of your networking efforts. Now, when we hear the term ROI, we usually think of financial returns, like how much profit we're making from an investment. But when it comes to networking, ROI isn't just about money—it's about *value*. Specifically, the value your connections are bringing to your career, business, personal growth and to the people you are connecting with.

In simple terms, networking ROI is about asking: "Is the time, energy, and effort I'm putting into networking worth it? Am I getting something meaningful in return?"

Why Evaluating Networking ROI Matters

You might be thinking, "Why should I evaluate my networking efforts? Isn't it just about meeting people and building connections?" While that's part of it, evaluating ROI is crucial because it helps you understand *how effective* your networking really is. It allows you to measure whether your efforts are leading to concrete results or if you're spending time and energy without seeing much benefit.

Here's why evaluating ROI matters:

1. **Resource Allocation: Are You Using Your Time Wisely?** Time is one of your most valuable resources. By evaluating your networking ROI, you can determine whether the time you're spending on events, meetings, and conversations is actually paying off. Are the connections you're making leading to new job opportunities, partnerships, or collaborations? If not, you might need to rethink where you're focusing your networking energy.

2. **Strategic Adjustments: What's Working and What's Not?** Evaluating ROI helps you figure out which networking strategies are working and which aren't. Maybe attending large conferences isn't leading to many useful contacts, but small, focused industry events are. Or perhaps reaching out to new connections on LinkedIn isn't paying off, but having in-person coffee meetings is. Once you know what's working, you can shift your focus to the strategies that deliver the best results.

3. **Identifying Success: Are You Reaching Your Goals?** When you know how to measure success in networking, you can build on what's working. Are your efforts leading to valuable opportunities, like meeting a mentor, landing a client, or learning from a key industry player? Evaluating your networking ROI helps you identify these wins so that you can keep doing more of what's effective.

How to Evaluate Networking ROI

So how do you actually measure the return on your networking efforts? Here are some simple, practical methods:

Track Opportunities That Come From Networking

One of the best ways to measure your networking ROI is by tracking the opportunities that come directly from your efforts. This could include job offers, new clients, collaborations, partnerships, or even speaking engagements.

How to do it:

- Keep a log or spreadsheet of every opportunity that comes from your networking activities.

- Note who the connection is, how you met them (at a conference, through LinkedIn, etc.), and what opportunity resulted (like a job lead or a client referral).

- Over time, you'll start to see patterns, helping you understand which networking efforts are the most valuable.

Assess the Strength of Your Relationships

Not all networking results in immediate job offers or partnerships, but building strong, valuable relationships is equally important. Evaluate the depth of your connections. Are you staying in touch with the people you meet? Are they reaching out to you for advice or collaboration? Strong relationships are often long-term investments that pay off down the line.

How to do it:

- Review your connections and ask yourself: Are they becoming more than just LinkedIn contacts? Are they evolving into mentors, collaborators, or trusted advisors?

- If you're getting to know people on a deeper level and staying in touch, you're building valuable long-term relationships—another indicator of positive networking ROI.

Compare the Time Invested to the Benefits Gained

This step is about balancing effort with results. If you're spending hours every month attending networking events or sending follow-up emails but aren't seeing any real benefits (new contacts, opportunities, or insights), it might be time to reconsider your approach.

How to do it:

- Write down how much time you're spending on different networking activities—whether it's attending events, sending emails, or scheduling meetings.

- Then, compare that to the tangible outcomes you've achieved. If the benefits aren't matching the time invested, you may need to adjust your focus to more productive networking strategies.

Summary:

Remember, the ultimate goal of networking is to create meaningful relationships that benefit your career or business in the long run. Evaluating your networking ROI helps you ensure that your time and energy are going to the right places. You'll have a clearer sense of what's working, what needs to change, and how you can continue building a network that delivers value over time.

Networking is a long-term investment. The relationships you build today may not provide immediate results, but over time, they can lead to new opportunities, collaborations, and growth. By setting clear goals, tracking your progress, and evaluating the return on your efforts, you'll maximize the value of your networking activities.

Networking is not about just connecting people. It's about connecting people with people, people with ideas, and people with opportunities.

Michele Jennae

CHAPTER 10

THE HEART OF NETWORKING

From the basics of building connections to advanced strategies for fostering partnerships, this book has been your guide to navigating the often-intimidating world of networking. But here's the thing: networking isn't just a tool for your career—it's a vital part of your personal and professional life, one that touches every aspect of growth, learning, and connection.

Throughout these chapters, we've discussed practical strategies for how to approach people, build genuine relationships, and even evaluate the return on your networking efforts. But the true value of networking goes beyond business deals, job opportunities, or career milestones. It's about cultivating relationships that enrich your life in unexpected ways, offering support, guidance, and even friendship. Networking isn't a one-time event—it's an ongoing process, one that, if nurtured, can offer lifelong benefits.

A Moment of Reflection:

As you continue networking journey (for now), take a moment to ask yourself a few key questions. Go ahead—be honest. This is where the real growth happens.

1. **How Have I Grown?** Think back to when you started this book. Were you nervous at the idea of walking into a networking event, or unsure of how to reach out to new contacts? Now, you've got the confidence and strategies to not just attend, but to leave an impression. How has your perception of networking evolved along the way?

2. **What's My Next Move?** Networking is about taking action. What's the first thing you're going to do after reading this? Will you reconnect with an old contact, attend a virtual event, or simply send a thoughtful email? Remember, the best networks are built one step at a time—so what will be yours?

3. **What Value Can I Bring to Others?** Who in your circle could use a helpful introduction, a piece of advice, or a listening ear? Remember, the best relationships are those that are built on mutual support.

4. **Am I Ready to Step Outside My Comfort Zone?** Let's be honest— growth never happens in your comfort zone. What's one thing that still makes you a little nervous? Is it approaching that industry leader or speaking up in a virtual discussion? It's time to push those boundaries because the magic happens just beyond them.

5. **Who Do I Want to Become?** This one's a little deeper. Who is the future version of you? A thought leader? A mentor? A trusted connection in your industry? Take a moment to envision that person—and then, think about the steps you can take today to grow into that role

A Continuous Process of Growth

As you continue to cultivate these connections, remember that networking isn't about instant gratification. It's about building relationships over time, offering value to others, and being open to what you can learn along the way. Like any other skill, networking improves with practice and patience. It's not about how many contacts you collect or how many events you attend—it's about the depth of the relationships you form and the opportunities you create for yourself and others.

Networking is a continuous process of growth. You will make mistakes along the way—maybe you'll fumble through introductions or send a follow-up email that doesn't get a response. That's okay. Each experience is an opportunity to learn and improve. The key is to keep showing up, to keep reaching out, and to trust that the relationships you're building now will lead to incredible things down the road.

Your Personal Networking Toolkit

This book is here for you as a guide, a support system as you navigate the often unpredictable world of networking. When you feel stuck or unsure of how to approach a new situation, come back to these pages. Revisit the basics if you need a refresher on how to make those initial connections. Return to the sections on building strategic partnerships or evaluating your ROI if you're ready to take your efforts to the next level. This isn't a one-time read; it's a resource you can turn to whenever you need it.

Final Tip: The Top Five Networking Habits for Long-Term Success

As you embark on the next steps of your networking journey, here are five habits to cultivate that will ensure your long-term success:

Be Proactive:

Don't wait for opportunities to come to you—seek them out. Reach out to people, attend events, and actively participate in conversations. The more you put yourself out there, the more chances you'll create for meaningful connections.

Listen More Than You Speak:

Networking isn't just about telling people who you are; it's about learning who they are. Ask questions, show interest, and listen deeply. People remember those who take the time to understand them.

Follow Up Consistently:

The key to building lasting relationships is in the follow-up. Whether it's a quick email after an event or checking in with a connection a few months down the line, staying in touch keeps you on their radar and reinforces the relationship.

Offer Value:

Always look for ways to give before you get. Whether it's sharing a useful resource, making an introduction, or offering your support, adding value to others' lives is the foundation of a strong network.

Be Patient and Persistent:

Networking is a long game. You won't always see results immediately, and that's okay. Keep investing in your relationships, keep nurturing your connections, and trust that the rewards will come over time.

A Lifelong Journey

The connections you build today will support you in ways you can't yet predict, enriching not just your professional path but your personal one as well. Whether you're seeking mentorship, business growth, or simply new perspectives, remember that networking is about building a community around you. One that will help you learn, grow, and thrive in every area of your life.

So, as you close this book, take these lessons with you. Put them into practice, adapt them to your unique journey, and trust that the relationships you cultivate will guide you toward your goals and beyond.

Here's to your continued success, your evolving connections, and the endless opportunities ahead. Happy networking!

ADDITIONAL RESOURCES & WORKSHEETS

To continue growing and refining your approach, this chapter offers a curated selection of further reading, online resources, and practical tools to keep you inspired and equipped for long-term success.

Think of these resources as your support system as you move forward. Whether you're looking to deepen relationships, explore new networking opportunities, or simply stay sharp in your professional interactions, these tools will help guide you along the way. Networking doesn't stop here—it evolves with you, and these resources are designed to ensure you're ready for every step of that journey.

Take what you've learned, apply it with intention, and use these additional resources to keep building a network that will continue to grow with you, both in your career and in your personal life.

Recommended Reading:

"Never Eat Alone" by Keith Ferrazzi

A classic in the world of networking, this book breaks down the mindset and tactics that have helped Ferrazzi build a vast and influential network. It focuses on the importance of generosity and creating authentic, lasting relationships.

"The Tipping Point" by Malcolm Gladwell

While not directly about networking, Gladwell's exploration of how small actions can lead to large-scale changes offers valuable insights for anyone looking to understand the impact of personal connections.

"Give and Take" **by Adam Grant**

This book focuses on the power of giving and how helping others can lead to greater success in both life and business. It's a great read for those looking to deepen their understanding of ethical networking and long-term relationship building.

"Crucial Conversations: Tools for Talking When Stakes Are High" **by Al Switzler, Joseph Grenny, and Ron McMillan**

Networking often involves high-stakes conversations where relationships, opportunities, or reputations are on the line. This book provides valuable strategies for navigating these situations with clarity and confidence.

"How to Win Friends and Influence People" **by Dale Carnegie**

A timeless guide to building relationships, Carnegie's book offers practical advice on how to make meaningful connections with people in both your personal and professional life.

Online Courses & Tools:

LinkedIn Learning

An excellent platform with a variety of courses on networking, communication, and personal branding. You'll find specific modules dedicated to building strategic partnerships and growing your network in digital spaces.

Coursera - Networking Basics for Career Success

This course offers insights into the fundamental principles of networking, with a focus on practical applications in a variety of professional settings.

X (formerly Twitter)

For those looking to build their digital presence and engage in real-time discussions, X is a valuable tool for interacting with influencers, sharing insights, and contributing to industry conversations.

Slack Communities

Many industries and professional groups have dedicated Slack communities where you can interact with peers, share ideas, and expand your network. Look for communities that align with your goals and interests.

Eventbrite

Discover local and virtual networking events in your area. Eventbrite offers a wide range of professional gatherings, from small meetups to large conferences, making it easy to find opportunities that fit your interests.

Networking Tools

Calendly

Scheduling meetings can be a hassle, especially when coordinating with busy professionals. Calendly allows you to share your availability and let others book time with you easily, eliminating the back-and-forth.

HubSpot CRM

Keeping track of your networking connections is essential for maintaining relationships. HubSpot offers a free CRM that allows you to manage your contacts, track interactions, and set reminders for follow-ups.

Loom

For a more personal touch in your networking, Loom allows you to record short video messages. This can be a unique way to follow up with someone after a meeting or event, making your outreach stand out.

Linktree

Linktree allows you to share multiple links from your social media bio or email signature, making it easier for others to access your portfolio, LinkedIn, and website with a single click.

REFLECTION WORKSHEETS

NETWORKING EVENT SELF-REFLECTION WORKSHEET

So, you've attended your first networking event—congrats! Or maybe you've been to a few but haven't quite nailed the interaction part yet. Either way, we're here to help you reflect and grow. Networking is like building muscle: it gets easier and stronger with time and practice. So, let's dive in and see how things went!

1. **What went well?** *(Celebrate the wins! Pick any that apply or write your own.)*

   ☐   I introduced myself confidently.

   ☐   I asked insightful questions and kept the conversation going.

   ☐   I remembered to follow up with someone I met.

   ☐   I wasn't too nervous to approach new people (even if it was just one person!).

   ☐   I shared something valuable or insightful.

   ☐   Other: _____

   ----

2. **What could I have done better?** *(Growth time! There's always something to improve. Check the ones that apply or add your own.)*

☐   I could have approached more people instead of sticking to the ones I knew.

☐   I felt unprepared or unsure of what to say.

☐   I dominated the conversation instead of listening more.

☐   I didn't follow up after the event.

☐   I felt out of place and didn't engage much.

☐   Other: _____

---

3. **Did I feel left out or uncomfortable approaching people?** *(This is common, don't worry! Let's figure out how you felt and how to tackle it next time.)*

☐   Yes, I felt left out and didn't know how to join conversations.

☐   Yes, I wanted to approach people but felt too nervous.

☐   No, I felt comfortable but didn't approach as many people as I'd like.

☐   No, I was able to jump into conversations without too much trouble.

---

4. **How can I overcome this next time?** *(Let's plan for future greatness! Choose one or more strategies to help you out.)*

   ☐ Prepare a few conversation starters or questions ahead of time.

   ☐ Focus on approaching one person at a time instead of groups.

   ☐ Remind myself that everyone is there to meet new people — just like me.

   ☐ Set a goal to approach at least 2-3 new people next time.

   ☐ Other: _____

---

5. **Do better next time.** *(What's one thing you'll commit to improving next time? Check the box or write in your goal.)*

   ☐ I will follow up with at least one new contact after the event.

   ☐ I will introduce myself to people outside my usual circle.

   ☐ I will focus on being an active listener rather than just talking.

   ☐ Other: _____

BEING A GIVER REFLECTION WORKSHEET

If you remember, we've spoken about the importance of being a giver in your network. Networking isn't just about what others can do for you—it's also about what you can offer them. Building a reputation as a "giver" means helping others without expecting anything in return. Whether it's sharing resources, connecting people, or offering advice, being generous with your time and knowledge is key to building strong, lasting relationships. Let's reflect on how you've been adding value and how you can do even more for the people in your network.

1. **How have I added value to my network recently?** *(Let's give yourself some credit! Check all the ways you've contributed or write in your own.)*

   ☐   I introduced two people who could benefit from knowing each other.

   ☐   I shared a useful article, tool, or resource with someone in my network.

   ☐   I offered advice or feedback to a colleague or connection.

   ☐   I recommended someone for an opportunity (job, project, partnership, etc.).

   ☐   I supported someone by attending their event, promoting their work, or giving encouragement.

   ☐   Other: _____

----

2. **What more could I do to add value to my network?** *(Time to think big! What's one more thing you could do to be a giver?)*

   ☐ Introduce a connection to someone who could help them professionally.

   ☐ Offer to review someone's work or give feedback.

   ☐ Share a resource or tool that could be useful to others.

   ☐ Send a note of encouragement or congratulations to someone on a recent achievement.

   ☐ Other: _____

   ----

3. **Who in my network could use a little support right now?** *(Take a moment to think of someone who might benefit from your help.)*

   ☐ A colleague looking for new job opportunities.

   ☐ A friend working on a new project or business.

   ☐ A peer trying to learn a new skill or break into a new industry.

   ☐ Someone who's been quiet lately—maybe they need a check-in or a friendly ear.

   ☐ Other: _____

   ----

4. **What's one action I can take this week to be a giver?** *(Let's set a goal! Choose a simple way to give back to someone in your network this week.)*

   ☐ I will introduce two people who could benefit from knowing each other.

   ☐ I will send an article or resource to someone who might find it useful.

   ☐ I will offer my advice or expertise to someone who needs help.

   ☐ I will attend or promote an event or project for someone in my network.

   ☐ Other: _____

   ----

5. **Reflecting on generosity: How does being a giver make me feel?** *(Let's take a moment to think about how your acts of generosity impact both you and others.)*

   ☐ It makes me feel more connected and engaged with my network.

   ☐ It feels good to help others succeed.

   ☐ It builds trust and strengthens my relationships.

   ☐ It encourages me to think of new ways to offer value.

   ☐ Other: _____

Ready for the final worksheet on time management?

TIME MANAGEMENT FOR NETWORKING WORKSHEET

Time is a precious resource, especially when you're juggling work, personal life, and your professional growth. If you remember, we talked about balancing your time when it comes to networking. The good news? You don't have to choose between building your network and getting other things done. It's all about smart time management. Let's dive into how you can maximize your networking efforts without feeling overwhelmed.

1. **How much time am I dedicating to networking each week?** *(Let's see where you're at! Choose the option that best matches your current efforts.)*

   ☐ Less than an hour (networking? What networking?).

   ☐ 1-3 hours (I'm getting the hang of it!).

   ☐ 4-6 hours (I've got networking penciled in like a pro).

   ☐ 7+ hours (I practically live on LinkedIn).

   ----

2. **Am I making the most of my networking time?** *(Honesty check! Are you using your time wisely or just scrolling? Pick what applies.)*

   ☐ Yes, I'm intentional with who I connect with and follow up regularly.

   ☐ Kind of, but I could be more focused in my approach.

☐ Not really, I tend to browse social media without much direction.

☐ No, I struggle to carve out consistent time for networking.

----

3. **What's my go-to strategy for balancing networking with other responsibilities?** *(You've got a busy schedule! What strategies work for you—or could work?)*

☐ I set aside specific time slots each week for networking.

☐ I integrate networking into my existing tasks (e.g., following up after meetings).

☐ I use tools like CRM systems or apps to stay organized.

☐ I haven't figured out a strategy yet, but I'm working on it.

----

4. **Where can I cut back to free up time for high-value connections?** *(There's always a way to trim the fat. What can you streamline or let go of to make room for quality networking?)*

☐ Spending less time on social media without a clear purpose.

☐ Limiting long email threads and moving to quicker calls or messages.

☐ Cutting back on events that don't align with my goals.

☐ Delegating some tasks to free up more time.

☐ Other: _____

----

5. **What's my time management goal for the next networking event?** *(Let's set a goal to make sure your next event is productive without taking over your schedule.)*

☐ I will spend no more than 30 minutes preparing before the event.

☐ I will connect with 3-5 people instead of trying to meet everyone.

☐ I will set follow-up reminders for connections within 24 hours.

☐ I will schedule a break to recharge during the event.

☐ Other: _____

----

6. **What can I automate or simplify to make networking easier?** *(Consider what tools or systems can help you streamline your efforts.)*

☐ I can use a CRM to track my contacts and follow-ups.

☐ I can schedule automated reminders to reconnect with people.

☐   I can batch my networking tasks (e.g., sending follow-up emails in one sitting).

☐   Other: _____

Congratulations! You've made it through the reflections and strategies that will help elevate your networking game. Whether it's reflecting on how to improve your approach at events, becoming a giver within your network, or managing your time wisely, you now have the tools to build genuine, valuable connections that last.

Remember, networking isn't about quick wins or transactional exchanges—it's about creating a foundation of trust, mutual respect, and long-term relationships. With the insights you've gained, you're not just adding people to your contacts; you're building a community that will support your growth and success.

As you move forward, remember: The key to networking is consistency, authenticity, and generosity. You don't have to do it all at once. Take it one step at a time, applying these strategies and reflecting as you go. Before you know it, you'll be thriving in a network full of meaningful connections, ready to help you achieve your goals.

Thank you for taking this journey through networking with me. Now, go out there and connect with confidence—you've got this!

ABOUT THE AUTHOR

Laureen Regan has over 35 years of expertise in founding, growing, and leading multiple successful B2B ventures. With a deep understanding of business development and strategic leadership, she has honed the art of cultivating meaningful professional relationships that drive sustained growth. Through her leadership in developing innovative business solutions and fostering cross-industry collaborations, Laureen has successfully created networks and partnerships that have spanned industries and borders.

Her vast experience extends beyond just starting and scaling businesses; Laureen has been instrumental in guiding companies to build lasting B2B relationships that deliver long-term value. Whether leading trade missions or crafting high-level business development strategies, she has consistently leveraged her network to create mutual benefit and enduring partnerships.

In **"Networking Mastery,"** Laureen shares practical insights and proven strategies from her career to help others master the art of networking, making her an ideal guide for anyone looking to build impactful, professional connections that elevate their career.

Made in the USA
Coppell, TX
25 November 2024

40909168R00085